POV Press
Books by Bethanne Kim

Survival Skills for All Ages

    #1: 26 Basic Life Skills

    #2: 52⁺ Everyday Recipes for Emergencies

    #3: 26 Mental and Urban Life Skills

Scouting in the Deep End:

    #1: Cubmastering

    #2: Leader of the Pack

    #3: Citizenship in the World

Not the Zombies

    #1: OMG!

    #2: BRB!

    Undead Swept Away

The Constitution: It's the OS for the US

The Organized Wedding: Planning Everything from Your Engagement to Your Marriage

Forthcoming:

Survival Skills for All Ages:

    26 Outdoor Life Skills

Special Needs Prepping

THE ORGANIZED WEDDING:

PLANNING EVERYTHING FROM YOUR ENGAGEMENT TO YOUR MARRIAGE

BETHANNE KIM

Cover Photo courtesy of My Vintage Vogue.

www.MyVintageVogue.com

ISBN: 978-1-942533-08-5

Distributed by POV Press
PO Box 399
Catharpin, VA 20143

Printed in the United States of America.

DEDICATION

To my beloved husband.

Table of Contents

CONTENTS

CONTENTS

ACKNOWLEDGMENTS

Thank you to my husband for his support and encouragement in writing this, and to my children for their tolerance while I edited this. Without them, this book certainly wouldn't exist.

Foreword

Dear Reader:

When my husband and I got married, I spent a year planning our wedding. It was attended by 150 of our friends and relatives, and our parents' friends and co-workers[1]. Our wedding day was lots of fun, but it took lots of work to pull it all together.

When we got engaged, my husband and I knew some of what was required to plan a wedding ceremony, reception and honeymoon, but we needed to learn a lot more. Some of it was in the wedding planners we found but a lot wasn't, especially for the ceremony and honeymoon. Those books were also too heavy and bulky to carry with us while we planned the biggest party of our lives, and too floral to leave out at work.

This planner provides a lot of information, hopefully without overwhelming you. It's

----

[1] Meeting new people (often your parents' co-workers and relatives you thought died years ago) at your wedding is so common it should be considered a tradition. Be prepared for a long list of people your parents are sure "must be" invited but that you don't know. Just try to convince them to limit it and accept meeting some new people. If they weren't proud of you, they wouldn't want their entire office at your wedding.

organized it so you can find everything quickly. To achieve all this, each section has a short introduction followed by hints and tips for saving time and money, then by checklists to help you take care of all the important details.

There are even recommendations for home security precautions during your honeymoon. It's easy to forget to have a friend pick up packages (wedding gifts!) from USPS, FedEx and UPS or forward / hold packages so they aren't returned to sender.

We had a Protestant ceremony, but this book doesn't assume that you will. That is why we refer to your "officiant" — not pastor, priest, rabbi, or judge — and "ceremony site" — not church, synagogue, or courthouse. Although there will clearly be differences depending on your religion, many things are similar for any type of wedding. For example, if you have a religious officiant, you will probably need to be counseled before they will marry you. You will also need to select appropriate (non-secular) ceremony music (not just the processional and recessional) and readings.

Compromise is integral to planning a wedding, especially if someone else is paying for it. While it is *your* wedding, you will still need to consider other people's wishes, budgetary and dietary restrictions, and both sets of family traditions. When you start planning, ask each set of parents if there is anything they strongly feel should be included in your wedding and include it, if possible.

You and your fiancé should decide what you feel strongly about and tell your families that you won't compromise on those items. Parents can feel that they have the right to make all the major decisions, especially if they pay for everything, potentially making it more difficult to get *your* dream wedding instead of *their* dream wedding.

Most importantly, remember that although you do need to consider other people, it is **your** wedding. Do what is most important to the two of you. Don't let a bossy photographer cut short your dinner because the lighting is "just right" outside if food is important to you. And don't let a caterer intimidate you into finishing dinner and missing the "perfect lighting" if photos are very important to you. And if you love chocolate cake, get a double-double chocolate cake with fudge frosting. Just don't drop it on the bride's gown. (You can always get a white groom's cake.)

Try to remember that even if they deliver the wrong cake, the limo driver is a no-show, there's a monsoon, and the band plays music you hate, _you will still have just married the person of your dreams!!!_

Isn't that what the whole thing is really about?

Wishing you all the best,

Bethanne Kim

Glossary

Bride's Cake: The traditional white, layered cake. It no longer "has to be" either white, which doesn't rise well, or layered.

Bridesmaid's Luncheon: A small celebration in honor of your bridesmaids and all the help they've given you. Both mothers are invited. A trip to a day spa is a popular alternative.

Bulletin/Program: Handed out at the ceremony, they list the attendants and family, ceremony order, and any special notes from the couple.

Cash Bar: Your guests pay for all or most of their drinks. You can also provide one drink (e.g., margaritas or beer) and have guests pay for everything else. See Open Bar.

Groom's Cake: A smaller cake in a shape or flavor reflecting the groom's interests (e.g., a golf scene or fraternity letters). Definitely optional.

Honor Attendant: For the bride, the maid or matron of honor. For the groom, the best man.

Host/Hostess: The person you designate to handle any problems during the wedding and reception. This may be one of your parents.

Officiant: The person who marries you. This can be a pastor, priest, rabbi, judge, "Chapel of Love" owner, or any other person recognized by the state you are marrying in.

Open Bar: You pay for everything your guests drink. See Cash Bar.

Processional: Music played as the bride and her attendants go down the aisle.

Receiving Line: The couple and their parents greet each guest as they walk through a line. It can take a long time, but may be the only chance to talk to some guests. May include honor attendants.

Recessional: Music played as the new couple and their attendants go back the aisle.

Registry: A gift wish list. The couple selects a few stores with registries, then spends several hours selecting the dishes, towels, picture frames, etc. they want to use for the next few decades. Have fun!

Rehearsal Dinner: Usually held after the rehearsal, all ceremony participants and out-of-town guests who have arrived are invited. Invitations are informal and attendants' gifts may be given out here. This can be a formal dinner or a barbecue - whatever you want.

Response Cards: Pre-addressed cards stamped and mailed in your wedding invitations. Guests write their name on the card inside and indicate if they will be attending and how many will be in their party. For sit-down meals, guests also indicate which menu choice they prefer.

Stationery: The paper products needed for a wedding – invitations, response cards, personalized napkins/matchbooks, and so much more!

Table Assignments: An exceptionally painful process, this is when you decide who will sit next to whom at the reception. The advantage is that you can make certain that your friends are at the same table, not with your parents' coworkers. The disadvantage is that it takes time. If you have table assignments, you need to have place cards and a place card table. It's usually worth the effort, but check with both sets of parents to find out which feuding relatives should be separated.

Thermography: Engraving was the standard for wedding invitations. Today, thermography successfully imitates the appearance of engraving for a lot less money.

Toss Bouquet: Instead of throwing the expensive bouquet they have put so much time and money into, brides may buy a toss bouquet. It is a much smaller version of her bouquet. Of course, some brides skip the toss altogether, but both the bouquet and garter toss are fun for kids.

Ushers: Usually men, they escort guests to their seat prior to the wedding ceremony. Groomsmen are often the ushers too. You should have one usher for every 50 guests.[2]

---

[2] Note: The following items are only used in Jewish weddings: Huppot and poles, Kiddush cup, Ketubah, Yarmulkes, Kittel, and glasses to break.

Superstitions and Traditions

- .. Something old, something new, something borrowed, and something blue, and a silver sixpence in your shoe. This tradition dates from the late 1900s.

- .. It's bad luck for the groom to see the bride before their wedding on their wedding day. (Personally, I think this is because the soon-to-be-married are often quite tense and could start arguing over nothing and ruin their wedding.) This is a Victorian tradition.

- .. It's bad luck to receive a knife as a gift. Include a penny as payment in thank you notes for knives.

- .. First time (and only first time) brides must wear white. Brides started wearing white in the eighteenth century, but it wasn't until the Victorian era that a "white wedding" became de rigeur.

- .. Attendants dress alike to confuse evil spirits. Thousands of years old.

- .. Rice is thrown to buy off cranky spirits. Hundreds of years old.

- .. Wedding rings are worn on the ring finger of the left hand because the vein in this finger was believed to go directly to the heart. Thousands of years old.

<u>Notes</u>

Key Telephone Numbers

☐.......Baby-sitter _____

☐.......Baker _____

☐.......Band/DJ _____

☐.......Best Man _____

☐.......Bridal store/alteration shop _____

☐.......Bridesmaids' gown store_____

☐.......Caterer _____

☐.......Ceremony site_____

☐.......County Clerk (for marriage license) _____

☐☐..Doctor (general practitioner) _____

☐.......Florist_____

☐.......Hair stylist_____

☐.......Honeymoon hotel _____

☐.......Hotel for out-of-town guests _____

☐.......Jeweler _____

☐.......Limo company _____

☐.......Maid of Honor _____

☐.......Make-up artist _____

☐.......Manicurist _____

☐.......OB/Gyn_____

☐ ......Officiant _____

☐ ......Organist/other musician_____

☐ ......Parents – Hers _____

☐ ......Parents – His _____

☐ ......Pet kennel _____

☐ ......Photographer_____

☐ ......Reception site _____

☐ ......Registry #1_____

   Registry Number _____

☐ ......Registry #2_____

   Registry Number _____

☐ ......Rental company (tables, etc.) _____

☐ ......Rehearsal dinner location _____

☐ ......Soloist _____

☐ ......Travel agent_____

☐ ......Tuxedo rental _____

☐ ......Videographer_____

☐ ......Wedding coordinator_____

☐ ......Wedding night hotel _____

Basic Information

Try to make the major decisions, including vendors, at least nine months before your wedding. Most of the good ones book up at least that far in advance. Finish everything that can be done in advance by two months before your wedding. Obviously, some things (table assignments, packing) can't be done until just before the wedding but if you get everything else done in advance, you'll be able to fully enjoy the last weeks before your wedding.

There are a few things you should do one year in advance to find in-season items. Most importantly, as soon as you decide your colors, both your mothers should start shopping for their dresses. The Bride's mother chooses her gown first, then the Groom's mother coordinates with her dress. The mothers should discuss the colors and styles they want to wear so they coordinate.

There are several To-Do Lists for specific people. One is for the Groom and includes the things they traditionally do. The other two are for the Bride and Groom's mothers. They are totally blank, beyond choosing a dress. You need to figure out what you are comfortable having them do. They want to make sure everything goes perfectly, and they want to be involved in the planning. They might even know a few things that are helpful for you. If you select areas that you want their help in, and are clear about areas that you and your fiancé want to decide yourselves, hopefully it will reduce some tension.

Since my Mom is a church organist, she was in charge of selecting an organist. As I told her, I had no opinion on that subject – it was her call. If you let your mothers help in areas they care (or know) about more than you do, they might stop trying to "help" in areas where you really don't want it. It can also free up some of your time to devote to things you care about more. When they start really bugging you, remember that they have been dreaming about (or possibly dreading) this day since before you were born. Whichever it was, they just want it to be perfect.

If your fiancé is not involved enough with planning your wedding, you might be overwhelming them with details. (Hasn't the whole process occasionally overwhelmed you?) Don't ask about things you know they *really* won't care about. My husband didn't know when we ordered a cake knife set, much less care what it looked like.

For areas you truly need help with, try narrowing the options and giving them three you like so they can't pick the wrong one. For example, I couldn't decide between two processional songs I loved so my husband chose.

When most people think of a wedding party, they think of the maid/matron of honor, bridesmaids, groomsmen, flower girl, ring bearer, bride and groom. In addition to these people, you can include Junior Bridesmaids, Junior Groomsmen, and ushers who are not groomsmen. Groomsmen stand up front during the ceremony. Ushers seat people. Groomsmen are often ushers too, but it's up to you. (As a rule of thumb, you should have one usher for every fifty guests.) Both sets of parents are also part of the bridal party.

Aside from the wedding party, you can ask friends to help with your wedding in a variety of ways. Examples include a guest book attendant, acolyte, reader and Huppot pole bearer. Although these people are not technically part of the Wedding Party (and therefore get out of the multi-hour photo shoots), they do help things run more smoothly.

There is a lot of information your wedding party needs to have. In fact, there's an entire checklist devoted to just this. There's a second checklist to remind you to send the information to everyone who needs it. You should also give everyone in your bridal party a list of exactly what you expect them to do in your wedding. Don't assume they know it all.

There are pages reminding you to record what you bought for each person as a thank-you gift and how much you paid. This will help to jog your memory so that you don't inadvertently spend a lot more/less on one person.

Hints and Tips

- If you live in or near a city with a central flower market, go look at their flowers. You may find new ones that you love for your wedding. Try to look 12 months ahead to find in-season flowers.

- If you live in or near a city with a garment district, look for a headpiece and veil there. It's less expensive.

- If you need something on your wedding day, ask someone for help. It might take you 20 minutes to get a glass of water, or a guest could bring it to you in two minutes. Most people will understand and be glad to help.

- Possible ways to limit the guest list include not having children (under 16 or 18?), coworkers, dates for single guests, or distant relatives.

- Before mailing response cards, write the guest's name on the back (or number the guest list and put the corresponding number) so you know who is responding, even if they forget to write their name.

- If you find a vintage gown that's a little tight, try a bustier/corset. Custom ones can suck you in where the gown is tight. This can be very cost effective compared to buying a new gown.

- You will be showing off your engagement and wedding rings on your wedding day. You can have a jeweler clean your engagement ring just before your wedding. You can also buy a small high-quality brush and use dish-detergent to clean it yourself in five minutes. (This recommendation is from a jeweler.)

- Your Honor Attendants (Maid/Matron of Honor and Best Man) should be at least 21 years old because they are the legal witnesses who sign your marriage certificate. Alternatively, you may designate another attendant to serve as your official witness.

- Your attendants and anyone else who is particularly helpful with your wedding is usually given a thank-you gift.

Considerations for setting a date:

- The peak season for weddings is April through October, causing intense competition for resources.

- What is your favorite season? What special dates do the two of you have?

- Does either family already have any conflicting events planned – trips, reunions, graduations?

- Avoid busy-season at work, because it will always be busy-season on your anniversary.

- Consider how heavy travel days and holidays will impact guests who live far away.

Newspaper Announcements:

- Review it before publication.

- Usually made by the parents of the bride not more than one year in advance.

- Gives the couple's names, their parent's names and the wedding date. May also ask where they were educated/degrees received, where they live, and current occupation and employer.

- Usually sent to the lifestyle or society editor of the local paper. A fee may be charged to print it.

Registering

- If you register more than six months in advance, items may be discontinued or you may select seasonal items your guests won't be able to find.

- Select two or three stores and register before your first shower. It's a good idea to make sure at least one is a national chain.

- Make sure the stores have branches convenient to your guests. Check return/exchange policies.

- You can register for more than dishes and linens. Power drills, mortgages, and more are available on registries. Include a few expensive gifts for groups who pool their money to buy a large gift.

- Include inexpensive items too. There are some really good slotted spoons, pizza cutters, etc. available. Each item is only a few dollars, but a full set can be costly.

- Tell your family and attendants where you register. They tell everyone else. Do not put this information in shower or wedding invitations.

- There is a multi-page gift recorder at the end of this book for your wedding gifts. When you open the bulk of your gifts after your wedding, have a few friends over for a small party. That way, they can record who gave you what as you open your gifts.

Bridal Shower:

- Held at least two weeks before your wedding. Informal, they can be co-ed and may have a theme (barbecue, kitchen, lingerie, linen).

- The bride is often involved in scheduling her shower. You may have several.

- You will need a gift recorder. Have an attendant or other friend record who gave you what in the "Engagement and Shower Gift Recorder" at the end of this book, or on a pad of paper.

- **If guests attend multiple showers, they are not expected to give multiple gifts.**

- Even if the shower is at your parents' home, they should not be the official hosts. Your honor attendant should be.

<u>Notes</u>

Budget

Bride's Priorities

Think about what **really** matters to you and number this list accordingly. It should help you figure out the budget and where other people can "help."

☐.......Ceremony Site_____

  ☐.......Unity Candle_____

  ☐.......Huppot, Kiddush Cup _____

☐.......Musician(s):

  ☐......Soloist_____

  ☐.......Ceremony Musician(s) _____

  ☐.......Reception Band/DJ _____

☐.......Photographer _____

☐......Videographer _____

☐☐..Bachelorette Party/Bridesmaids Lunch _____

☐.......Rehearsal Dinner _____

☐.......Reception Site _____

☐.......Food & Beverages:

  ☐.......Appetizers_____

  ☐.......Entrees _____

  ☐☐..Cake (primary, Groom's) _____

  ☐.......Drinks/Bar _____

☐.......Rental items (tables, chairs, etc.) _____

☐ ......Favors _____

☐ ......Guest Book_____

☐ ......Bird seed/Bubbles _____

☐ ......Invitations _____

    ☐ ......Calligraphy _____

☐ ......Limousine _____

☐ ......Flowers:

    ☐ ......Bridal Bouquet _____

    ☐ ......Attendants _____

    ☐ ......Parents/Special Guests _____

    ☐ ......Ceremony Site_____

    ☐ ......Reception Site _____

☐ ......Bridal Beauty:

    ☐ ......Gown _____

    ☐ ......Headpiece/Veil_____

    ☐ ......Petticoat/Bustier_____

    ☐ ......Jewelry _____

    ☐ ......Shoes_____

    ☐☐ .Going-away outfit (his and hers) _____

    ☐☐ .Hair stylist, make-up _____

☐ ......Tuxedo and Accessories _____

☐ ......Honeymoon_____

Groom's Priorities

Think about what **really** matters to you and number this list accordingly. It should help you figure out the budget and where other people can "help."

☐.......Ceremony Site_____

    ☐.......Unity Candle_____

    ☐.......Huppot, Kiddush Cup _____

☐.......Musician(s):

    ☐.......Soloist_____

    ☐.......Ceremony Musician(s) _____

    ☐.......Reception Band/DJ _____

☐.......Photographer _____

☐.......Videographer _____

☐.......Bachelor Party_____

☐.......Rehearsal Dinner _____

☐.......Reception Site _____

☐.......Food & Beverages:

    ☐.......Appetizers_____

    ☐.......Entrees _____

    ☐☐..Cake (Primary, Groom's) _____

    ☐.......Drinks/Bar _____

☐.......Rental items (tables, chairs, etc.) _____

☐.......Favors_____

☐ ......Guest Book_____

☐ ......Bird seed/Bubbles _____

☐ ......Invitations _____

      ☐ ......Calligraphy _____

☐ ......Limousine _____

☐ ......Flowers:

      ☐ ......Bridal Bouquet _____

      ☐ ...... Attendants _____

      ☐ ......Parents/Special Guests _____

      ☐ ......Ceremony Site_____

      ☐ ......Reception Site _____

☐ ......Bridal Beauty:

      ☐ ......Gown _____

      ☐ ......Headpiece/Veil_____

      ☐ ......Petticoat/Bustier_____

      ☐ ......Jewelry _____

      ☐ ......Shoes_____

      ☐☐ .Going-away outfits (his and hers) ____

      ☐ ......Hair stylist _____

      ☐ ......Make-up_____

☐ ......Tuxedo and Accessories _____

☐ ......Honeymoon_____

Who Pays for What

Traditionally, the bride's parents paid for the wedding, the grooms' for the honeymoon, and the couple received gifts. Today, who pays for what is as unique as you and your families.

☐......Ceremony site_____

       ☐☐..Officiant, counseling donation_____

       ☐.......Janitor and misc. fees_____

☐......Marriage license _____

       ☐.......Blood tests _____

       ☐.......Medical examination _____

☐......Reception site _____

☐......Caterer _____

☐......Rented items (tables, chairs)_____

☐......Coordinator_____

☐......Florist _____

☐......Photographer _____

☐......Videographer _____

☐......Organist/ceremony musician _____

☐......Soloist_____

☐......DJ/band_____

☐......Rehearsal dinner _____

_____

☐ ......Bridal lunch _____

☐ ......Hotel rooms for bridal party _____

☐ ......Bridesmaid's gifts _____

☐ ......Groomsmen's gifts _____

☐ ......Yarmulkes, Kittel _____

☐ ......Huppot _____

☐☐ .Glasses - to break and for toasting _____

☐ ......Kiddush cup _____

☐ ......Ketubah _____

☐☐ .Limousine and parking _____

☐ ......Bride's cake _____

☐ ......Groom's cake_____

☐ ......Favors _____

☐ ......Guest book_____

☐ ......Birdseed/bubbles _____

☐ ......Coat check _____

☐☐ .Bar and bartender_____

☐ ......Restroom attendant _____

☐ ......Police officer _____

☐☐ .Wedding bands_____

_____

☐........Wedding gown_____

   ☐........Alterations_____

   ☐........Headpiece _____

   ☐........Hoop/petticoat_____

   ☐........Undergarments_____

   ☐........Jewelry_____

   ☐........Trousseau _____

   ☐........Going away outfit _____

   ☐☐..Clean and preserve wedding gown __

☐........Beauty appointments:

   ☐........Hair stylist_____

   ☐........Make-up artist _____

   ☐........Manicure/pedicure _____

☐........Misc. small stuff _____

☐........Tuxedo rental _____

☐........Groom's accessories_____

☐☐..Invitations and announcements_____

☐........Calligraphy _____

☐........Postage for invitations_____

☐........Thank you notes and postage _____

☐☐..Airfare to wedding _____

☐........Hotel the night before the wedding _____

☐ ......Wedding night hotel room _____

☐ ......Honeymoon_____

    ☐ ......Airfare _____

    ☐ ......Hotels _____

    ☐ ......Car rental _____

    ☐ ......Special event tickets _____

_____

_____

_____

_____

_____

_____

_____

_____

_____

Totals:

    Bride's Parents: $_____

    Bride: $ _____

    Groom's Parents: $ _____

    Groom: $_____

Payments Made

If there are two check blocks, the first is for the first payment, the second is for the final payment.

☐.......Reserve ceremony site _____

$.........._____

☐.......Janitor's fee (ceremony site) _____

$.........._____

☐☐..Officiant's fee / counseling donation _____

$.........._____

☐.......Organist/ceremony musician _____

$.........._____

☐.......Soloist_____

$.........._____

☐.......Limousine _____

$.........._____

☐☐..Wedding gown and alterations _____

$.........._____

$.........._____

☐☐..Tuxedo rental _____

$.........._____

$.........._____

☐.......Rehearsal dinner site _____

$ .... _____

☐☐ .Reception site _____

$ .... _____

$ .... _____

☐☐ .Band/DJ_____

$ .... _____

$ .... _____

☐☐ .Photographer_____

$ .... _____

$ .... _____

☐☐ .Videographer_____

$ .... _____

$ .... _____

☐☐ .Baker _____

$ .... _____

$ .... _____

☐☐ .Caterer _____

$ .... _____

$ .... _____

☐☐ .Rental company (chairs, tables, etc.) _____

$ .... _____

$ .... _____

To-Do Lists

Groom

☐.......Select attendants and ask them. I know one man who asked his friends two weeks before the wedding. You MUST do it earlier than that! _____

☐.......Select ushers and ask them. One per 50 guests; they can be groomsmen also. _____

☐.......Select tux store and style. _____

☐.......Free tux rental for groom with other rentals?

☐.......Men's shoes (rented? loafers? patent leather?)

☐.......Get tux measurements_____

☐☐..Get groomsmen to send their measurements to the tux shop by_____

      ☐.......Send in your own measurements ____

☐.......See doctor for check-up and blood test. _____

☐.......Prepare guest list._____

☐☐..Tell parents how many guests they may invite and make them stick to it or pay for extras. __

_____

☐.......Plan rehearsal dinner with your parents.____

☐☐☐..Arrange transportation to ceremony, reception, and honeymoon. _____

☐☐..Buy wedding bands with fiancé. _____

☐☐.Have wedding bands engraved. _____

☐☐.Check marriage license requirements. Set time with fiancé to get it, then get and keep track of it. Some states waive the minimum wait if you live out of state and request one with a good excuse, like insufficient vacation to fly back early._____

☐......Buy a wedding gift for your fiancé. _____

☐☐.Order boutonnieres, pay for bride's bouquet.

☐......Tell attendants wedding and rehearsal details. _____

☐......Buy thank you gifts for your attendants. _____

☐......Make moving arrangements. _____

☐.....Talk to your family about problems._____

☐......Plan honeymoon and wedding night hotel.__

☐☐.Update passport, get visas (his & hers)

☐......Buy traveler's checks._____

☐......Locate ATMs for your honeymoon.___

☐......Double-check honeymoon reservations, confirmation numbers._____

If your fiancé wants you to help select something (like invitations) but the selection overwhelms you, ask them to narrow down the selection to a manageable number - just be clear whether manageable means twelve or three. And write thank you notes.

Bride's Mother

☐.......Select your gown. Tell the groom's mother what color you will be wearing so she can coordinate _____

_____

_____

_____

_____

_____

_____

_____

_____

_____

_____

_____

_____

_____

_____

_____

_____

_____

_____

_____

_____

_____

_____

_____

_____

_____

_____

_____

_____

_____

_____

_____

_____

_____

Groom's Mother

☐.......Find out what color the Bride's mother is wearing and buy a dress that coordinates with it___

_____

_____

_____

_____

_____

_____

_____

_____

_____

_____

_____

_____

_____

_____

_____

_____

_____

_____

_____

_____

_____

_____

_____

_____

_____

_____

_____

_____

_____

_____

Attendants

Attendants are expected to pay for the purchase or rental of their wedding day clothing.

You may include the adults in the receiving line, but that is optional.

After the Mother of the Bride is seated, all the Groomsmen and Junior Groomsmen move to the right front (as you face the front) of the ceremony site with the Groom. The Groom stands closest to the center with the Best Man to his right. The Groomsmen and then Junior Groomsmen stand to the right of the Best Man.

For the Processional, the Junior Bridesmaids go first, followed by the Bridesmaids. The Maid/Matron of Honor fixes the Bride's train and veil during this time. She goes after the Bridesmaids. The Ring Bearer may go right before the Flower Girl or walk down with her. The Flower Girl goes last. There is either a new piece of music or a change in tempo in the processional, then the Bride and her Father/Escort go down the aisle.

Your officiant will tell you exactly where to stand, but generally the Bride is closest to the center with the Maid/Matron of Honor to her left, then her Bridesmaids and Junior Bridesmaids. The exact location of the Ring Bearer and Flower Girl varies a great deal, particularly during the ceremony.

There is no rule about which Bridesmaid or

Groomsman stand closest to the couple. You could arrange them by height, gown color (if you let each select a flattering color), how long you've known them, or any other order you want. You can also try to match the heights of Groomsmen and Bridesmaids.

Maid/Matron of Honor:

- Help with pre-wedding jobs, particularly addressing invitations and running errands.

- Plan and hostess a Bridal Shower with the other bridesmaids at least two weeks before the wedding. Bridal Showers used to be surprises, but it is now often necessary to coordinate with the Bride.

- Record shower and wedding gifts (optional). A Bridesmaid or other friend may also do this.

- Arrange for a Bachelorette Party, if desired.

- Arrive early for pictures and to help the bride dress. Remind her to eat something and use the restroom before dressing. Guess who gets to help when she needs to go to the restroom in all her bridal finery….

- For double-ring ceremonies, hold the Groom's ring until the appropriate point in the ceremony.

- Arrange the bride's train and veil as needed and bustle her train before the reception.

- Hold the bride's flowers as needed.

- Sign the wedding certificate as a witness. If she is not at least 21, designate another attendant as a witness.

- Make a toast at the reception (optional).

Bridesmaids:

- Help Bride with pre-wedding jobs, including addressing invitations.

- Help arrange a Bridal Shower.

- Record shower and wedding gifts (optional).

- Arrive early for pictures.

Junior Bridesmaids:

- Usually age eight to sixteen

- Dress in a similar style to adult Bridesmaids.

- May attend pre-wedding parties and showers.

Flower Girls:

- Usually two to seven years old.

- May sprinkle flower petals for the Bride to walk on. She may also just carry a small bouquet and look cute.

Best Man:

- Help the Groom with pre-wedding jobs.

- Arrange the Bachelor Party (if any).

- Drive the Groom to the church prior to the ceremony.

- Hold the Bride's ring and Marriage Certificate until the appropriate point in the ceremony.

- Sign the wedding certificate as a witness. If he is not at least 21, designate another attendant as a witness.

- Pay the officiant and other vendors (chauffeur, reception site) after the wedding. The Groom should give him labeled envelopes with checks for everyone who needs paid no later than the rehearsal dinner.

- Make the first toast at the reception.

- Arrange for the newlywed's honeymoon departure.

- Return rental tuxes to the tux shop. Someone else may do this, especially if the Best Man is from out of town.

Groomsmen:

- Perform all Usher duties (below).

- Arrive at the wedding location early and help set up.

- Seat guests of honor last (Bride's and Groom's parents, grandparents), in the pews reserved for them. The first pew or two on each side is saved for immediate family. The Bride's side goes on the left side, facing the front. The Groom's family goes on the right.

- Escort Bridesmaids.

- Direct guests at the reception.

- Move gifts to a safe location after the wedding.

Ushers:

- Give bulletins/programs to guests as they arrive and seat them. In the past, the Bride's friends and families sat on one side and the Groom's on the other. Today, guests are usually seated on the side with more space when they arrive.

- If you have Ushers who are not Groomsmen, they can seat late-arriving guests and put the aisle runner down for the Bride. This lets the Groomsmen stay up front with the Groom the entire time.

- The Head Usher (or Best Man) escorts the Mother of the Bride to her pew. She is the last one to be seated and this officially starts the wedding processional.

Junior Groomsmen:

- Dress in a style similar to adult Groomsmen.

- Usually age eight to sixteen.

Ring Bearers:

- Carry a pillow with fake ring(s) on it. The Honor Attendants have the real ones so they aren't dropped and lost.

- Usually two to seven years old.

- Be cute.

Bridal Party

Both sets of parents are part of the bridal party.

☐.......Maid/Matron of Honor _____

☐.......Bridesmaid #1_____

☐.......Bridesmaid #2_____

☐.......Bridesmaid #3_____

☐.......Bridesmaid #4_____

☐.......Bridesmaid #5_____

☐.......Jr. Bridesmaid #1 _____

☐.......Jr. Bridesmaid #2 _____

☐.......Flower girl #1 _____

☐.......Flower girl #2 _____

☐.......Best Man _____

☐.......Groomsman #1_____

☐.......Groomsman #2_____

☐.......Groomsman #3_____

☐.......Groomsman #4_____

☐.......Groomsman #5_____

☐.......Usher #1 _____

☐.......Usher #2 _____

☐.......Usher #3 _____

☐ ......Jr. Groomsman #1_____

☐ ......Jr. Groomsman #2_____

☐ ......Ring bearer_____

☐ ......Escort bride down the aisle. Traditionally, this is the father of the bride. _____

_____

_____

_____

_____

_____

_____

_____

_____

_____

_____

_____

_____

_____

_____

Additional Assistants

☐☐☐...Acolytes/altar boys _____

☐.......Reader(s) _____

☐.......Bulletin/program/mass book distribution __

_____

☐.......Birdseed/bubble distribution _____

☐☐..Seating his mother (step mother)_____

☐☐..Seating her mother (step mother) _____

☐.......Ring pillow arrangements (watch ring bearer) _____

☐.......Remove unity candle, Kiddush cup, etc. from ceremony site _____

☐.......Reception Host/Hostess_____

☐.......Arrange placecards _____

☐.......Set up gift table_____

☐.......Reception set-up (take over cake knife, etc.) _

_____

☐.......Collect leftover favors _____

☐.......Final walk-through of ceremony and reception sites to check for forgotten items (incl. dressing rooms) _____

_____

☐ ......Take wedding gown to dry cleaners _____

☐ ......Store wedding gifts until after honeymoon __

☐ ......House-sitter _____

☐ ......Pet-sitter/kennel_____

☐ ......Baby-sitter _____

☐ ......Send bridal bouquet for preservation _____

☐ ......Pay:

    ☐ ......Officiant _____

    ☐ ......Organist _____

    ☐ ......Soloist _____

    ☐ ......Reception site _____

    ☐ ......Band/DJ_____

_____

☐ ......Return rented tuxes _____

☐ ......Return other rentals (tables, etc.) _____

_____

☐ ......Move and store top cake layer _____

☐ ......Retrieve gift money and deposit in bank ____

☐ ......Church secretary. Send a thank you note if he

or she typed up or copied your bulletins. _____

_____

Thank You Gifts

Are any of your attendants' <u>really</u> short of space in their home? Do any have children or pets who might damage delicate gifts? What hobbies or interests do they have? Keep those things in mind when selecting gifts.

- Bookends

- Movie – romance like "Sleepless in Seattle"?

- Book

- Gift Certificate

- Keychain or money clip

- Picture Frame

- Engraved item

- Really good make-up brushes

- Music

- Tickets to a concert/show

- Toys (Lego can be a BIG hit with adults)

- Jewelry (cufflinks for men; women's can coordinate with their bridesmaids' gowns)

- Something related to your wedding - for a wedding near the Amish, hex signs or quilted pillows; at Walt Disney World, try something with Mickey Mouse

- Potted plants

- Perfume/cologne

- Stationery

- Jewelry / music box

- Snowglobe

- Travel or shaving kit

- Computer or board game (especially for kids)

- Good pen set or fountain pen

- Framed photo of you with your attendant

- Gift basket of scented soaps, etc.

- Something from their favorite sports team

- Something from their college/university

- Spa visit / certificate

- Something related to their interests

- A toy from Sharper Image, Brookstone or a similar store (very different from Toy 'r' Us toys)

- Still stuck? Check out gadget stores like Herrington and Hammacher Schlemmer, museum shops like the Smithsonian and the New York Metropolitan Museum of Art, or hobby companies like Bits & Pieces (puzzles) and the Gourmet Chef.

_____

_____

Thank You Gifts

This is a REALLY long list. You probably won't buy gifts for this many people. They're just reminders.

☐☐..His parents _____

$.........._____

☐☐..Her parents _____

$.........._____

☐.......Maid of Honor _____

$.........._____

☐.......Bridesmaid #1_____

$.........._____

☐.......Bridesmaid #2_____

$.........._____

☐.......Bridesmaid #3_____

$.........._____

☐.......Bridesmaid #4_____

$.........._____

☐.......Bridesmaid #5_____

$.........._____

☐.......Best Man _____

$.........._____

_____

☐ ......Groomsman #1 _____

    $ .... _____

☐ ......Groomsman #2 _____

    $ .... _____

☐ ......Groomsman #3 _____

    $ .... _____

☐ ......Groomsman #4 _____

    $ .... _____

☐ ......Groomsman #5 _____

    $ .... _____

☐ ......Usher #1 _____

    $ .... _____

☐ ......Usher #2 _____

    $ .... _____

☐ ......Usher #3 _____

    $ .... _____

☐ ......Jr. Bridesmaid #1 _____

    $ .... _____

☐ ......Jr. Bridesmaid #2 _____

    $ .... _____

☐ ......Flower girl #1 _____

    $ .... _____

☐.......Flower girl #2 _____

    $.........._____

☐.......Jr. Groomsman #1 _____

    $.........._____

☐.......Jr. Groomsman #2 _____

    $.........._____

☐.......Ring bearer _____

    $.........._____

☐.......Reader _____

    $.........._____

☐.......Reception set-up (take over cake knife, etc.) _

    $.........._____

☐.......Reception Host/Hostess_____

    $.........._____

☐.......House-sitter_____

    $.........._____

☐.......Pet watcher _____

    $.........._____

_____

_____

_____

_____

_____

_____

_____

_____

_____

_____

_____

_____

_____

_____

_____

_____

_____

_____

_____

_____

_____

Wedding Party Information Packets

☐.......Date, time, and exact ceremony location; approximate arrival time and location for bridal party (usually when photos start for men, when the bride gets dressed for women); expected end time of the reception.

_____

☐.......Date, time, exact location, and dress code for the rehearsal and rehearsal dinner _____

☐.......Date, time, location of other parties _____

_____

☐.......Directions:

    ☐.......Hotel_____

    ☐.......Ceremony site (incl. from hotel) _____

    ☐.......Rehearsal dinner _____

    ☐.......Reception_____

☐.......Job description, tasks you want them to do. Best Man gives a short toast, groomsmen seat people, etc._____

_____

☐.......Men only:

    ☐.......Tux shop address/email_____

    ☐.......Send in tux measurements by _____

    ☐.......Deposit of $___, final payment of $___

(Are checks accepted for final payment?) ____

☐ ......Shoes (rent? black patent? specifics?) _

☐ ......Pick up tuxes by_____on _____

☐ ......Time/place to arrive for photos _____

☐ ......Time to start seating guests_____

☐ ......Who will return tuxes to tux shop? When do they get them? (At the reception? after party?) _____

☐ ......Women only:

    ☐ ......Dress store address/email_____

    ☐ ......Send in measurements by _____

    ☐ ......Pick up dress by _____

    ☐ ......Complete alterations by_____

    ☐ ......Shoes (Dyed? Color? Height?) _____

    ☐ ......Stocking color _____

    ☐ ......Hair/headpiece style _____

    ☐ ......Jewelry _____

    ☐ ......Time/place to arrive before ceremony to help bride dress _____

☐ ......Hotel location and phone number _____

☐ ......Registries. You're supposed to tell them. ____

Wedding Party Information Packets Sent

☐.......Wedding coordinator _____

☐.......Officiant _____

☐.......Cantor _____

☐☐..His Parents _____

☐☐..Her Parents _____

☐.......Maid of Honor _____

☐.......Bridesmaid #1 _____

☐.......Bridesmaid #2 _____

☐.......Bridesmaid #3 _____

☐.......Bridesmaid #4 _____

☐.......Bridesmaid #5 _____

☐.......Jr. Bridesmaid #1 _____

☐.......Jr. Bridesmaid #2 _____

☐.......Flower girl #1 _____

☐.......Flower girl #2 _____

☐.......Best Man _____

☐.......Groomsman #1 _____

☐.......Groomsman #2 _____

☐.......Groomsman #3 _____

☐.......Groomsman #4 _____

☐ ......Groomsman #5 _____

☐ ......Usher #1 _____

☐ ......Usher #2_____

☐ ......Usher #3_____

☐ ......Jr. Groomsman #1_____

☐ ......Jr. Groomsman #2_____

☐ ......Ring bearer_____

☐ ......Acolytes/altar boys _____

_____

☐ ......Reader_____

☐ ......Reception Host/Hostess _____

☐ ......Reception set-up (take over cake knife, etc.) _

_____

☐ ......Organist. The soloist and organist normally meet on their own and only the organist attends the rehearsal. The organist may charge a fee to attend; it is worth it. If the soloist attends, send them a packet._____

_____

☐ ......Other_____

_____

_____

Ceremony and Reception

The marriage ceremony is when you actually become husband and wife. The reception and everything else is a celebration of the marriage ceremony. If you read enough bridal books, you may forget that anything happens between getting dressed and the post-ceremony photo shoot. Your officiant is the best guide for your ceremony.

If you are getting married in a house of worship (church, synagogue, etc.), your wedding is automatically a *private religious service*. Because it is a religious service, there are usually restrictions on photography, videography, music and other areas your officiant will advise you of. These can be frustrating, but your officiant is not trying to be difficult. They are following their beliefs. Everyone must follow the same restrictions. For example, some pastors only officiate inside a church. Outside "in God's Creation" is not the same to them.

Of course, it's often easier to find a church or synagogue to be married in and to get the time you want than to find a secular site, and much easier than a reception site. Discuss requirements and restrictions with your officiant early in the planning process. Areas to talk about include counseling requirements; if you must both be baptized; and restrictions on: photography (flash allowed?), videography (stationary or moving?), music (only one secular piece, or more?), flowers (must you leave them for Sabbath services?), birdseed or bubbles, and the receiving line location.

Protestant ceremonies often provide bulletins (programs) explaining who is in the bridal party and giving special notes from the couple. Even if you don't use a bulletin or program, this is a handy list of important details.

If you are getting married or having your reception outside, buy nice sunglasses. You'll probably be wearing them in a lot of your pictures.

If you have more than about 100 guests, you should seriously consider having a receiving line. You probably won't have another chance to talk to some of your guests. Also, I hate to say this, but you may never see some of them again. Just keep the line to your parents and the two of you.

Financially, having an open bar (you pay for everything) or a cash bar (guests pay) is a major consideration. It is possible to compromise on this by providing a few drinks (a keg of beer, champagne punch, margaritas, soda) and having a cash bar for all other alcohol. You can also limit how long drinks are served.[3]

If you have specific dietary restrictions, including kosher needs or allergies, be very clear about this

---

[3] Lawsuits are also a consideration. Limiting how long drinks are served means that there is more time between when guests drink and when they leave.

with the caterer. You should seriously consider having one vegetarian entrée (like pasta primavera) because there are so many vegetarians today.

Regarding your wedding cake: get your favorite flavor. The only questionable choice today is actually white. No one will be offended, but it doesn't rise nicely. You can even get a chocolate croquembouche – a chocolate covered craft base with pieces of chocolate stuck on with toothpicks. The major advantage to a yellow (or white) cake with white frosting is that it won't leave a big mark if you drop it on your gown.

We alternated layers of strawberry and yellow cake. We also had an ice cream sundae bar for dessert. Everyone loved them both. Also, if you don't want to freeze your top layer for a year, you could freeze it until your one-month anniversary or a similar date. We ate ours after our honeymoon, while we opened our gifts.

Hints and Tips

- Take your engagement ring off (or put it on another finger) before the actual wedding ceremony. Ask your Maid of Honor to remind you.

- Traditionally, the bride's friends and family sat on one side and the groom's on the other. Today, guests often sit on the side with more space when they arrive.

Ceremony site and officiant questions:

- What are the requirements - including counseling? How much is the usual donation for counseling?

- Are aisle runners, musical instruments, Huppot, or unity candleholders provided? What decorations are provided?

- Is tossing rice allowed? Many sites no longer allow rice to be tossed and couples need to use birdseed or bubbles instead.

- What are the restrictions on music?

- What restrictions are there for photographers and videographers?

- Are you expected to leave any of the flowers for Sabbath services?

- When can you access the site to decorate it? To prepare on your wedding day?

- Are there other weddings that day?

- Can you have a receiving line? Where?

- Cost for the ceremony? Janitorial service?

- Does your officiant want your marriage license at the rehearsal? If he takes it a day early, it's one less worry on your wedding day.

- Is there an electric stained glass window in the front of the church? If there is, it may be turned off at the same time as the candles. Have your acolyte (or officiant) turn it back on before any pictures are taken.

Reception site questions:

- Is there a discounted price or different menu for kids?

- How much do carafes of wine cost vs. bottles? Carafes are often cheaper.

About your reception:

- Many couples skip the bouquet and garter toss. Children enjoy trying to catch them. You can buy cheap ($2 or so) toss garters at craft stores.

- White cake doesn't rise nicely. Yellow is a better choice. So are chocolate and carrot.

- If your wedding is large, supplement your fancy wedding cake with a simple sheet cake that's cut in the kitchen.

- Buy some games for small children to play with at the reception. A piñata. Crayons and a coloring book. Inflatable musical instruments. Anything to entertain them after dinner is over.

- We typed up a one page "story" of our life together – how we met, places we liked to go on dates, how and where he proposed, meeting each other's families and our honeymoon plans. We copied them onto bond paper, rolled them up and gave one to each guest. It was a conversation starter and answered many common questions so we weren't telling the same few stories over and over. This gave us more time to talk to friends.

- If you write your story, roll the paper around a dowel rod. Use the inexpensive silver or gold "rings" sold in craft stores and bridal catalogs to hold them.

Bridal Beauty

☐.......Gown:

    ☐.......First alterations/dry clean 4 weeks before formal portrait, <u>at least</u> 3 months before the wedding _____

    ☐.......Final fitting _____

    ☐.......Picked up_____

    ☐.......Pressed and hung up_____

☐.......Petticoat/hoop _____

☐.......Undergarments_____

☐☐..Stockings, a spare pair, garter belt_____

☐☐..Headpiece and veil _____

☐.......Gloves _____

☐☐..Garters (one to keep, one to toss)_____

☐.......Shoes _____

☐.......Jacket/coat/cape _____

☐.......Bridal bag:

    ☐☐..Safety pins, bobbie pins_____

    ☐☐..Needle and thread _____

    ☐.......Spare stockings_____

    ☐.......Clear nail polish _____

    ☐.......Handkerchief _____

    ☐.......Contact lens/eye drops_____

☐ ......Contact lens case _____

☐ ......Hard candy/cough drops _____

☐ ......Sunscreen, sunglasses _____

☐ ......Advil/Tylenol _____

☐ ......Antihistamines _____

☐ ......Spare earring backs _____

☐ ......Small pad of paper and pen _____

☐ ......Extra camera memory _____

☐☐☐.Necklace, earrings, bracelet_____

☐ ......Sunglasses, check how they look with gown _

☐☐.Haircut (trial, and final appointment) _____

_____

☐☐.Make-up application (trial, final appointment)_____

_____

☐☐.Manicure and pedicure _____

☐ ......Going away outfit (with shoes and accessories) _____

_____

Thigh highs have solid strips of rubber at the top hold them up, not garters. It's easier to use the ladies room than with full nylons or gartered stockings. Try them before the wedding if you're interested but unsure. Good ones stay up for hours, even with dancing.

Bulletin/Program

☐.......Music (see separate sheet)_____

☐.......Participants (including their relationship):

    ☐.......Officiant_____

    ☐.......Cantor _____

    ☐.......Maid of Honor _____

    ☐.......Bridesmaid #1_____

    ☐.......Bridesmaid #2_____

    ☐.......Bridesmaid #3_____

    ☐.......Bridesmaid #4_____

    ☐.......Bridesmaid #5_____

    ☐.......Jr. Bridesmaid #1 _____

    ☐.......Jr. Bridesmaid #2 _____

    ☐.......Flower girl #1 _____

    ☐.......Flower girl #2 _____

    ☐.......Best Man _____

    ☐.......Groomsman #1_____

    ☐.......Groomsman #2_____

    ☐.......Groomsman #3_____

    ☐.......Groomsman #4_____

    ☐.......Groomsman #5_____

    ☐.......Usher #1 _____

    ☐.......Usher #2 _____

☐ ......Usher #3 _____

☐ ......Jr. Groomsman #1 _____

☐ ......Jr. Groomsman #2 _____

☐ ......Ring bearer _____

☐ ......Organist/ceremony musician _____

☐ ......Soloist _____

☐ ......Acolytes/altar boys _____

☐ ......Reader _____

☐ ......Bulletin/mass book distribution _____

☐ ......Birdseed/bubble distribution _____

☐☐ .His/her grandparents _____

☐☐ .His/her godparents _____

☐☐ .Readings:

_____

_____

☐ ......Special notes (e.g., bride's gown is an heirloom):

_____

_____

Christian bookstores sell blank bulletins. They cost *a lot* less than programs by invitation companies. Send thank you notes if someone types and copies them for you.

Music

Ceremony

☐.......OK selections with your ceremony site (churches often limit secular pieces) **and musician -** Do they know it? Can they learn it (for a price)? ___

☐.......Organist/other _____

    ☐.......Fee $ _____

☐.......Soloist _____

    ☐.......Fee $ _____

☐.......Other musician _____

    ☐.......Fee $ _____

☐.......Pre-ceremony (about 20 minutes). Many popular pre-ceremony pieces are only 2-3 minutes, so you'll need about six.

_____

_____

_____

_____

☐.......Solos (usually 2-3) _____

_____

_____

☐ Unity Candle Solo_____

☐ ......Processional_____

☐ ......Hymn _____

☐ ......Communion_____

☐ ......Recessional_____

_____

Reception

☐ ......Name of DJ/band_____

    ☐ ......Fee $ _____

☐ ......DJ/band start time_____; end time _____

☐ ......First dance _____

☐ ......Father/daughter dance _____

☐ ......Mother/son dance (or one parents' dance) __

☐ ......Garter toss (optional) _____

☐ ......Bouquet toss (optional) _____

☐ ......Start of money dance (optional) _____

☐ ......Last dance _____

_____

_____

In addition to bridal magazine and online lists of wedding music, some music stores (the kind that sell musicians sheet music) sell CDs full of them.

Musical Options

Ceremony
Pre-Ceremony
"So This Is Love" (Cinderella) - David, Hoffman, Livingston
"Ave Maria" - Schubert
"Jesu, Joy of Man's Desiring" - Bach
"Let Us Ever Walk With Jesus" - Gieschen
"Processional in 'C' " - Hopson
"Wedding Bells" - Peale
Processionals - can also be Pre-Ceremony Music
"Bridal Chorus" ("Lohengrin") - Wagner
"Canon in D" - Pachelbel
"Dance of the Sugar Plum Fairies" - Tchaikovsky
"Ode to Joy" - Beethoven
"Rondeau" ("Masterpiece Theater" theme) - Mouret
"Trumpet Tune" - Purcell
"Trumpet Voluntary" - Dupuis
"Trumpet Voluntary in 'D Major' " - Clarke
"Waltz of the Flowers" - Tchaikovsky
"Where'er You Walk (Semele)" - Handel
Solos - these can also be used for the Reception
"All I Ask of You" - Norbet and Callahan
"The Bride's Prayer" - Good
"God, a Woman and a Man" - Peele
"The Irish Wedding Song" - traditional
"The Lord's Prayer" - Malotte
"Now Thank We All Our God" - Bach
"Savior Like A Shepherd Lead Us" - Bradbury
"Simple Gifts" - Shaker Song
"Song of Ruth" - Eilers
"The Unity Candle Song" - Sullivan
"The Wedding Prayer" - Dunlap

"The Wedding Song" - Paul Stookey"

Recessionals - can also be Pre-Ceremony Music

"All Creatures of Our God and King" - Williams

"Alla Hornpipe" from "Water Music" - Handel

"The Arrival of the Queen of Sheba" - Handel

"Cantata No. 51 - Alleluia" - Bach

"Pomp and Circumstance" - Elgar

"Rondeau" ("Masterpiece Theater" theme) - Mouret

"Russian Dance" - Tchaikovsky

"Toccata Symphony V" - Widor

"Trumpet Tune" - Stanley

"Wedding March" ("Midsummer Night's Dream") - Mendelssohn

Reception

"All I Ask of You" - Michael Crawford

"As Time Goes By" - Irving Berlin

"Because You Loved Me" - Celine Dion

"Butterfly Kisses" - Bob Carlisle

"Daddy's Little Girl" - Burke and Gerlach

"Endless Love" - Diana Ross and Lionel Richie.

"Hopelessly Devoted to You" - Olivia Newton John

"I Swear" - J.M. Montgomery - All 4 One

"I Will Always Love You" - Whitney Houston

"Just the Way You Are" - Billy Joel

Frank Sinatra - anything he did

"Sunrise, Sunset" - from "Fiddler on the Roof"

"Time in a Bottle" - Jim Croce

"Unchained Melody" - Righteous Brothers

"Unforgettable" - Natalie Cole or Nat King Cole

"Up Where We Belong" - Joe Cocker, Jennifer Warnes

"Woman" - John Lennon

"Wonderful Tonight" - Eric Clapton

"You are the Sunshine of My Life" - Stevie Wonder

"We've Only Just Begun" - The Carpenters

Reception

Estimate #1

☐......Company Name _____

☐......Address _____

☐......Phone number (_____)_____

☐......Website _____

☐......Deposit of $____If cancelled, is it returned? _

☐......In-house caterer?____Must you use them? __

☐......Per person costs:

    ☐......Meals cost from $_____ to $ _____

    ☐......Drinks cost from $_____ to $ _____

☐......Is there a wine corkage fee? $_____

☐......Can you bring in your own cake? _____

Is there a cutting/serving fee? _____

☐......Minimum _____ and maximum number ____

☐......Number per table____ Dance floor size _____

☐......Times and dates available_____

Charges if you run overtime $ _____

When can you set-up/decorate site?_____

Other events at the site that day? _____

☐......Decorations available _____

☐......Is there a coatroom? $_____Bartender? $ ___

Doorman? $_____Ample parking? $ _____

Police/security? $_____Other charges $ _____

☐ ......When is a final count required? _____

_____

_____

_____

_____

Estimate #2

☐ ......Company Name _____

☐ ...... Address _____

☐ ......Phone number (_____) _____

☐ ......Website_____

☐ ......Deposit of $____If cancelled, is it returned? __

☐ ......In-house caterer?____Must you use them?___

☐ ......Per person costs:

    ☐ ......Meals cost from $_____ to $_____

    ☐ ......Drinks cost from $_____ to $_____

☐ ......Is there a wine corkage fee? $ _____

☐ ......Can you bring in your own cake? _____

Is there a cutting/serving fee? _____

☐ ......Minimum _____ and maximum number ____

☐.......Number per table____ Dance floor size _____

☐.......Times and dates available_____

Charges if you run overtime $ _____

When can you set-up/decorate site?_____

Other events at the site that day? _____

☐.......Decorations available _____

☐.......Is there a coatroom? $_____Bartender? $ ___

Doorman? $_____Ample parking? $_____

Police/security? $_____Other charges $_____

☐.......When is a final count required?_____

_____

_____

_____

_____

Estimate #3

☐.......Company Name_____

☐.......Address _____

☐.......Phone number (____)_____

☐.......Website _____

☐.......Deposit of $____If cancelled, is it returned? _

☐.......In-house caterer?____Must you use them? __

☐ ......Per person costs:

    ☐ ......Meals cost from $_____ to $_____

    ☐ ......Drinks cost from $_____ to $_____

☐ ......Is there a wine corkage fee? $ _____

☐ ......Can you bring in your own cake? _____

Is there a cutting/serving fee? _____

☐ ......Minimum _____ and maximum number ____

☐ ......Number per table____ Dance floor size _____

☐ ......Times and dates available _____

Charges if you run overtime $ _____

When can you set-up/decorate site?_____

Other events at the site that day?_____

☐ ......Decorations available _____

☐ ......Is there a coatroom? $_____Bartender? $ ___

Doorman? $_____Ample parking? $ _____

Police/security? $_____Other charges $ _____

☐ ......When is a final count required? _____

_____

_____

_____

_____

Menu/Reception Arrangements

Final count due on___Adults___Kids___Babies___

Meal #1_____ Meal #2_____Meal #3_____

Some reception sites charge less for children 4-11 years old, and even less for kids under 4, or offer a kids menu.

☐........Hors d'oeuvres (during photo shoot) _____

_____

☐........Appetizers (served with the meal) _____

_____

☐........Salad and dressing_____

☐........Entree #1 (Vegetarian)_____

_____

☐........Entree #2 _____

_____

☐........Entree #3 _____

_____

☐........Dessert_____

_____

☐........Kosher food - milchig (dairy) _____

         flayshig (meat) _____

☐ ......Cake flavor_____

☐ ......Punch flavor _____

☐ ......Bar (does site permit drinking? open? cash?)_

_____

☐ ......Drink for toasting _____

☐ ......Hours reception site is reserved for_____

_____

☐ ......Person(s) who will decorate site_____

☐ ......When can reception site be decorated? _____

_____

☐ ......Decorations _____

_____

☐ ......Will smoking be permitted? _____

☐ ......Wedding day contact for the reception site; give this name to the site. This person will handle problems so you and your spouse can enjoy your reception. _____

_____

☐ ......Person to bring drinks to bridal party during the photo shoot._____

☐ ......Restrictions to note_____

_____

Reception Decorations, etc.

☐.......Toasting glasses _____

☐.......Attendants' toasting glasses _____

☐.......Bouquet holder to clamp onto table _____

_____

☐.......Cake knife set _____

☐.......Cake boxes _____

☐.......Favors_____

_____

☐.......Napkins _____

☐.......Matchbooks_____

☐.......Thank you scrolls_____

_____

☐.......Basket or wishing well for cards. Have it watched so nothing is lost; some will have money inside. _____

_____

☐.......Table centerpieces. They don't need to be elaborate. You can have something simple like a single rose, baby's breath and a few non-Mylar balloons._____

_____

☐ ......Photos of you and your fiancé. It's affordable, a conversation starter for your guests, and your friends and family will probably enjoy looking at photos of you two having fun. _____

_____

_____

☐ ......Place cards _____

☐ ......Napkins rings _____

☐ ......After-dinner entertainment to keep kids occupied so grown-ups can visit longer – ad libs, dominos, maybe even a baby-sitter. _____

_____

_____

☐ ......Balloons _____

☐ ......Arch _____

☐ ......Potted trees, plants _____

☐ ......Fountain _____

☐ ......Lighted marquee _____

☐ ......Ice sculptures _____

☐ ......Candles _____

_____

_____

Reception Program

Before your wedding day, give a copy of this to your MC and a second copy to the person handling last-minute problems on your wedding day.

☐.......Reception starts _____

_____

☐.......Serve bridal party drinks during the photo shoot. _____

_____

☐.......Bride and groom arrive_____

_____

☐.......Introductions _____

_____

☐.......Receiving line _____

_____

☐.......Dinner served _____

_____

☐.......Blessing(s) _____

_____

☐.......Toast(s)_____

_____

☐ ......First dance _____

_____

☐ ......Father/daughter dance _____

_____

☐ ......Mother/son dance _____

_____

☐ ......Cake cutting_____

_____

☐ ......Bouquet toss _____

_____

☐ ......Garter toss _____

_____

☐ ......Money dance_____

_____

☐ ......Last dance _____

_____

☐ ......Bride and groom leave_____

_____

_____

_____

Rehearsal and Rehearsal Dinner

Rehearsal

☐.......Location_____

☐.......Directions to location_____

_____

_____

☐.......Time: from_____until _____

☐.......Payments for:

   ☐.......Ceremony site_____

   ☐.......Officiant_____

   ☐.......Organist/other musician _____

☐......."Bouquet" of ribbons from bridal shower ___

Ask ceremony site if you can leave the following after the rehearsal. If not, choose a friend to take care of them. This leaves less to worry about on your wedding day.

☐.......Bubbles/birdseed_____

☐.......Bulletins/programs _____

☐.......Guest book and pen_____

☐.......Unity candles (one pillar, two tapers), holder

☐☐..Marriage license, Ketubah (check with your officiant – some take them early so you can't forget)

☐.......Huppot and poles _____

☐ ...... Kiddush cup, glasses _____

☐ ...... Ring bearer's pillow _____

☐ ...... Flower girl's basket_____

☐ ...... Basket for birdseed _____

_____

_____

Rehearsal Dinner

☐ ...... Location _____

☐ ...... Directions to location _____

_____

☐ ...... Time: from_____until _____

☐ ...... Non-bridal party guests_____

_____

_____

☐ ...... Menu _____

_____

_____

_____

☐ ...... Distribute Thank-You Gifts_____

_____

Religious Ceremony

If you are married in a house of worship, your wedding is a religious service and you must follow certain guidelines, including limits on photography and secular music. Talk to your officiant to learn these rules.

☐.......Church/temple ("site") reserved_____

   ☐.......Address:_____

   ☐.......Phone number _____

_____

☐.......Counseling with officiant _____

☐.......Fees related to site use:

   ☐.......Officiant performing ceremony _____

   ☐.......Counseling by officiant _____

   ☐.......Site use_____

   ☐.......Janitorial service_____

   ☐.......Other _____

☐.......Site requirements/restrictions:

   ☐.......Music _____

   ☐.......Photography/videography _____

   ☐.......Flowers (where should they be delivered? are altar flowers to be left at the site?) _____

   ☐.......Bubbles/birdseed_____

☐ ......Other restrictions _____

☐ ......Readings selected - approved by officiant:

☐ ......Reading #1_____

☐ ......Reading #2_____

☐ ......If Biblical, version of the Bible. (King James uses thees and thous; Revised Standard – RSV – doesn't). Ask your officiant which is used. If you have a strong preference, provide your own Bible. _____

☐ ......Room for Bride/Groom to dress in _____

☐ ......Rehearsal time_____

☐ ......Sufficient reserved parking_____

☐ ......Is proof of baptism required? _____

☐ ......Color of the day (so you don't clash horribly)

☐ ......Homily (a mini-sermon) _____

☐ ......Kneeler _____

☐☐ .Crowns _____

☐☐ .Kiddush cup, cup for wine _____

☐☐ .Glasses to break w/napkin or pouch _____

☐ ......Huppot and poles_____

☐ ......Yarmulkes _____

☐ ......Kittel for groom_____

☐☐ .Ketubah, correct color pen _____

Remarriage

☐.......Things he wants to do, or skip. _____

_____

☐.......Things she wants to do, or skip. _____

_____

☐.......Is this a first wedding for one of you? _____

_____

☐.......Things you DO need/want to register for. __

_____

☐.......Things you DON'T need/want to register for

_____

☐.......His expectations for the wedding._____

_____

☐.......Her expectations for the wedding. _____

_____

☐.......His expectations for the marriage._____

_____

☐.......Her expectations for the marriage. _____

_____

_____

_____

_____

_____

_____

_____

_____

_____

_____

_____

_____

_____

_____

_____

_____

_____

_____

_____

_____

Involving Your Children

Some of these are for small children, others are for adult children.

☐.......Part of the unity candle ceremony. _____

_____

☐.......Part of the wedding party. _____

_____

☐.......Invited to all showers, pre-wedding parties.

_____

☐.......Submitted their guest list with a few friends.

_____

☐.......Selected/approved their wedding outfit. ___

_____

☐.......Have their own camera. _____

_____

☐.......Included in ceremony._____

_____

☐.......Special gift for them. _____

_____

_____

☐ ......Read a special selection._____

_____

☐ ......Have them make a drawing representing your wedding. Have it matted and have your guests sign the mat instead of a guest book. _____

_____

☐ ......About two weeks before your wedding, go out somewhere they really want to go and do something not related to the wedding. Don't bring your fiancé unless <u>your child</u> asks you to. _____

_____

☐ ......Listen to <u>their</u> concerns about <u>their</u> new step-

parent and other family changes _____

_____

_____

_____

_____

_____

_____

_____

_____

Honeymoon

Your honeymoon is an important part of your wedding. Have fun with it! If you plan your honeymoon yourself, it will be more work than using a travel agent, but you will have more control over the cost and can go exactly where you want to. Of course, experienced travel agents can help you find hidden jewels you might miss.

The first and most important step is to decide where you want to go. There are two pages for each of you to write the kinds of places you would go and things you would do on your ideal vacation. Often, the first place that comes to mind for a honeymoon is a nice, sunny island but that isn't everyone's ideal vacation. If you want to go kayaking or visit Bucharest, go for it!

Check the amenities at your hotel before packing. To my surprise, we needed bathing suits in October in England because the timeshare had an indoor pool and sauna. We also needed waterproof shoes and raincoats because it was still England.

No matter what you do, make sure you have plenty of time to rest so you aren't too tired for romantic evenings. Remember, it's your honeymoon! You'll take a lot more vacations together, so you can go back if you miss a few fun activities.

Hints and Tips

- If you buy lingerie a few months in advance, you can put it in a drawer or suitcase with a sachet. By your honeymoon, it should smell GREAT! If you do, then put a sheet of plastic wrap under the sachet--occasionally, oil from spices can leak and stain your things.

- If you go to a beach and one of you is fair, be very careful to always wear enough waterproof sunscreen, and be sure to reapply often. More than one person has had their honeymoon ruined by a bad sunburn.

- When making reservations, use the bride's maiden name because she won't have proof of her name change (if any) yet.

- Most credit cards have a pin number. You may need it to use your card outside of the USA.

- Search sites like Travelocity.com and PriceLine.com for the lowest possible airfare. Southwest.com is the exclusive online distributor for Southwest Airlines tickets.

- Hotels consider anything after 6 pm to be a late arrival. If you will arrive at your wedding night or honeymoon hotel(s) later than 6 pm, be sure to have your room(s) guaranteed for late arrival.

- You can locate nearby ATMs before leaving on your honeymoon by asking your bank for a listing or by searching online.

Car Rental

Domestic and International:

☐ ....Alamo   888-233-8749   Alamo.com _____

☐ ....Avis   800- 633-3469 Avis.com_____

☐ ....Budget   800-218-7992   Budget.com_____

☐ ....Dollar   800-800-4000   Dollar.com _____

☐ ....Enterprise 800-261-7331   Enterprise.com___

☐ ....Hertz   800-654-3131   Hertz.com_____

☐ ....National   800-501-9010   NationalCar.com_

☐ ....Thrifty   800-847-4389   Thrifty.com_____

Questions to ask:

☐ ....If one of you is under 25, is there a surcharge? _____

☐ ....Is the car stick or automatic? It's worth paying for automatic in left-side drive countries, and may not be a choice. _____

☐ ....Is the trunk covered? (esp. outside US) _____

☐ ....Is there an additional charge for your spouse to drive too? There usually isn't in the US, but may be in other countries. _____

☐ ....Where is the car pick up / drop off?_____

_____

☐ ....How long does it take to get from the car

drop-off point to the airport terminals and vice versa? _____

☐ ......If you arrive and depart from different places, is there a drop-off location closer to your destination? _____

_____

☐ ......Is there a courtesy shuttle to your hotel? ____

☐ ......Discounts available/used (AAA, your employer, airline tie-ins) _____

_____

☐ ......If you don't use a credit card, is a refundable cash deposit required? ($1,000+ isn't unusual) _____

☐ ......What is the minimum deposit taken from a credit card? You may end up close to your limit. ___

☐ ......Cost $_____for rental from _____until_____

    ☐ ......Cost with unlimited mileage is $ _____

    ☐ ......_____ miles free, $____ per extra mile

☐ ......Size car reserved _____

☐ ......Amenities requested (convertible?) _____

_____

☐☐ .Make and model of car reserved._____

☐ ......Cost/gallon if you don't top off the gas tank

_____

Potential Destinations

Good information sources include tourist boards, travel agents, travel books, and the Internet.

Type of Trip:

☐.......Cultural trip (another country, museums)___

☐.......Adventure (kayaking, skiing) _____

☐.......Educational (snorkeling, glass blowing) ____

☐.......Relaxation (the beach, a spa) _____

☐.......Cruise_____

Accommodations:

☐.......Bed and Breakfast _____

☐.......Hotel/motel _____

☐.......4 Star hotel_____

☐.......All inclusive resort_____

☐.......House or bungalow _____

Locale:

☐.......Mountains _____

☐.......Desert_____

☐.......Beach _____

☐.......City_____

☐.......Country _____

_____

Restrictions:

☐ ......Budget $ _____

☐ ......Start on_____, end on _____

☐ ......Minimum of ____days, maximum of ___days

☐ ......No travel via (boat, plane, etc.)_____

(due to motion sickness, phobias, etc.) _____

☐ ......Be within_____hours, _____miles of _____

☐ ......Speak these languages (international)_____

☐ ......Activities must include _____

_____

_____

Potential Destinations:

☐ ......Regions/countries _____

_____

☐ ......Cities_____

_____

_____

☐ ......Resorts _____

_____

_____

His Dream Vacation

If you could go anywhere, do anything on vacation, what would it be? Maybe climbing Mt. Everest is out of the question but mountain climbing lessons (or very long hikes) aren't. If you want to try French cooking but can't afford Europe, maybe Cajun cooking in New Orleans is for you. The idea is for to write down places you dream of going, then figure out what you would both enjoy and can realistically do. This is the place for wild ideas! Dream big!

Cities (domestic and international): _____

_____

_____

Countries: _____

_____

_____

Historical sites (Tower of London, Hollywood &

Vine):._____

_____

_____

Natural wonders (Mt. Everest, Grand Canyon): ____

_____

_____

Cultural sights (the Louvre, NFL Hall of Fame): ____

_____

_____

_____

Sports to try (rollerblading, mountain climbing): ___

_____

_____

_____

_____

Skills to learn (cooking, race car driving):_____

_____

_____

_____

Important vacation activities (sunbathing,):_____

_____

_____

_____

Restrictions (motion sickness, medical, phobias)____

_____

Her Dream Vacation

If you could go anywhere, do anything on vacation, what would it be? Maybe climbing Mt. Everest is out of the question but mountain climbing lessons (or very long hikes) aren't. If you want to try French cooking but can't afford Europe, maybe Cajun cooking in New Orleans is for you. The idea is for to write down places you dream of going, then figure out what you would both enjoy and can realistically do. This is the place for wild ideas! Dream big!

Cities (domestic and international): _____

_____

_____

Countries: _____

_____

_____

Historical sites (Versailles, the Alamo): _____

_____

_____

Natural wonders (Mt. Everest, Grand Canyon): ____

_____

_____

_____

Cultural sights (Grand Ole Opry, the Met in NYC): _

_____

_____

_____

Sports to try (scuba diving, skiing): _____

_____

_____

_____

_____

Skills to learn (massage, trapeze artist): _____

_____

_____

_____

Important vacation activities (sunbathing,): _____

_____

_____

_____

Restrictions (motion sickness, medical, phobias)____

_____

Final Plans

☐.......Destination _____

☐.......Travel agent _____

☐.......Airline and confirmation number _____

_____

☐.......Arrival date and time _____

_____

☐.......Departure date and time_____

_____

☐.......Rental car company and confirmation
number_____

_____

☐.......Wedding night hotel _____

      ☐.......Phone number _____

      ☐.......Website _____

      ☐.......Address _____

      ☐.......Confirmation number _____

☐.......Honeymoon hotel(s) _____

      ☐.......Phone number _____

      ☐.......Website _____

      ☐.......Address _____

      ☐.......Confirmation number _____

☐☐. Contact information given to:

☐☐. Family _____

☐☐. Assistants _____

☐ ...... Baby-sitter _____

☐ ...... Check if insurance is valid (esp. overseas):

☐ ...... Rental car. Read your credit card's fine print. You may be covered in the USA but not other countries. If you're insured in the USA, using that saves you money. If you go outside the USA, take the name and operator number of the person who confirmed coverage so you aren't charged VAT tax. ____

☐ ...... Floater policy for ring(s) valid _____

☐ ...... Health _____

☐ ...... Special cell phone use instructions (especially internationally) _____

☐☐. Vacation request submitted to employers ___

☐ ...... Registered for honeymoon (as a gift) at _____

_____

☐ ...... Local maps _____

_____

When you make reservations, you may need to use the bride's maiden name because she won't have proof of her name change (if any) yet.

Budget

☐.......Destination _____

☐.......From_____until_____

☐.......Airfare per person _____

☐.......Car rental w/mileage charges _____

☐.......Gasoline_____

☐.......Airport shuttles _____

☐.......Passports, Visas, Immunizations _____

☐.......Licenses, Permits _____

☐.......Subway/Underground/Metro passes _____

☐.......Other transportation (cabs, trains) _____

☐.......Room _____

☐.......Food per day (estimated) _____

_____

☐.......Admission tickets (museums, parks, etc.) ___

_____

☐.......Honeymoon Specials_____

☐.......Special events _____

_____

☐.......Restrictions (minimum stay) _____

_____

Final Estimate

☐ ...... Destination_____

☐ ...... From_____until _____

☐ ...... Airfare per person _____

☐ ...... Car rental w/mileage charges _____

☐ ...... Gasoline _____

☐ ...... Airport shuttles_____

☐ ...... Passports, Visas, Immunizations _____

☐ ...... Licenses, Permits_____

☐ ...... Subway/Underground/Metro passes _____

☐ ...... Other transportation (cabs, trains)_____

☐ ...... Room_____

☐ ...... Food per day (estimated)_____

_____

☐ ...... Admission tickets (museums, parks, etc.)____

_____

☐ ...... Honeymoon Specials _____

☐ ...... Special events _____

_____

☐ ...... Restrictions (minimum stay)_____

_____

First Estimate

☐.......Destination _____

☐.......From_____until_____

☐.......Airfare per person _____

☐.......Car rental w/mileage charges _____

☐.......Gasoline_____

☐.......Airport shuttles _____

☐.......Passports, Visas, Immunizations_____

☐.......Licenses, Permits _____

☐.......Subway/Underground/Metro passes _____

☐.......Other transportation (cabs, trains) _____

☐.......Room _____

☐.......Food per day (estimated) _____

_____

☐.......Admission tickets (museums, parks, etc.) ___

_____

☐.......Honeymoon Specials_____

☐.......Special events _____

_____

☐.......Restrictions (minimum stay) _____

_____

Second Estimate

☐ ...... Destination_____

☐ ...... From_____until _____

☐ ...... Airfare per person _____

☐ ...... Car rental w/mileage charges _____

☐ ...... Gasoline _____

☐ ...... Airport shuttles_____

☐ ...... Passports, Visas, Immunizations _____

☐ ...... Licenses, Permits_____

☐ ...... Subway/Underground/Metro passes _____

☐ ...... Other transportation (cabs, trains)_____

☐ ...... Room_____

☐ ...... Food per day (estimated)_____

_____

☐ ...... Admission tickets (museums, parks, etc.)____

_____

☐ ...... Honeymoon Specials _____

☐ ...... Special events _____

_____

☐ ...... Restrictions (minimum stay)_____

_____

Third Estimate

☐.......Destination _____

☐.......From_____until_____

☐.......Airfare per person _____

☐.......Car rental w/mileage charges _____

☐.......Gasoline_____

☐.......Airport shuttles _____

☐.......Passports, Visas, Immunizations _____

☐.......Licenses, Permits _____

☐.......Subway/Underground/Metro passes _____

☐.......Other transportation (cabs, trains) _____

☐.......Room _____

☐.......Food per day (estimated) _____

_____

☐.......Admission tickets (museums, parks, etc.) ___

_____

☐.......Honeymoon Specials_____

☐.......Special events _____

_____

☐.......Restrictions (minimum stay) _____

_____

Fourth Estimate

☐ ......Destination_____

☐ ......From_____until _____

☐ ......Airfare per person _____

☐ ......Car rental w/mileage charges _____

☐ ......Gasoline _____

☐ ......Airport shuttles_____

☐ ......Passports, Visas, Immunizations _____

☐ ......Licenses, Permits_____

☐ ......Subway/Underground/Metro passes _____

☐ ......Other transportation (cabs, trains)_____

☐ ......Room_____

☐ ......Food per day (estimated)_____

_____

☐ ......Admission tickets (museums, parks, etc.)____

_____

☐ ......Honeymoon Specials _____

☐ ......Special events _____

_____

☐ ......Restrictions (minimum stay)_____

_____

Getting Ready to Go

Home Security

☐☐..Have mail held starting_____ending ____

(Start a few days early to make sure it works.)

☐☐..UPS (800-742-5877), FedEx (800-463-3339) asked to hold or forward packages (gifts) from _____to _____

_____

☐.......Put a hold on delivery services (e.g., water) _

from_____until _____

☐☐..House watched by _____

    ☐.......Phone number _____

☐☐..Pets watched by _____

from_____until _____

    ☐.......Phone number _____

☐☐..Children baby-sat by _____

from_____until _____

    ☐.......Phone number _____

☐☐..Timers set on lights in these rooms: _____

_____

_____

_____

New timers have different settings for every day of the week or vary within 15 minutes of a set time to fool thieves. Confirm lights with timers aren't likely to fall over or be knocked (by pets) onto something flammable.

☐ ...... Valuables in safety deposit box at _____

☐ ...... Fireplace flue closed (for warmth) _____

☐ ...... Thermostat adjusted to save energy _____

☐ ...... Fix broken window or door locks _____

☐ ...... Blinds adjusted. If you normally leave them all down, keep them all down; if you normally have them at all different heights, keep them at different heights so it looks normal - just make sure there's nothing valuable visible. Hide that Faberge Egg collection! _____

_____

_____

_____

_____

_____

_____

_____

_____

International Travel

☐☐..Update passports two months before trip, by

_____ on_____

New passports cost more than renewals. You need two identical passport-size photos taken within the last six months, a birth certificate with a raised seal and a copy of your driver's license or other valid photo ID. It takes five or six weeks normally, but The National Passport Information Center can get you one in two weeks, for an extra fee. Large cities have passport centers with same-day service, for another fee. Some post offices accept applications.

☐.......Hers expires on_____

☐.......His expires on _____

☐☐..Get visas for both of you for (country and dates)._____

_____

_____

☐☐..Get passport photos for passports, 2 each, and visas, 2 per person per visa.

☐.......Need total of_____photos of her _____

☐.......Need total of_____photos of him_____

☐.......Credit card companies notified of international travel so they don't think it's stolen and cut off your card. _____

☐ ......Extra credit card in case of problems_____

☐ ......Buy $_____ in traveler's checks at _____

_____

☐ ......Buy travelers checks in foreign currency ____

AAA and some banks sell them to members.

☐ ......Closest ATMs to hotel are located at _____

_____

_____

☐ ......Restrictions on usage (do you need a 4 digit pin for international use?) _____

_____

☐☐ .Immunizations needed_____for _____

Most countries don't require them. _____

_____

☐ ......Check health conditions with the Centers for Disease Control for more unusual spots. _____

_____

☐ ......Check the US State Department web site (travel.state.gov) or travel advisory line for potential hazards._____

_____

_____

Packing

Financial and related:

☐.......His cell phone charger_____

☐.......Her cell phone charger _____

☐.......His laptop, tablet, Kindle and chargers _____

☐.......Her laptop, tablet, Kindle and chargers _____

☐☐..Cash and credit cards _____

☐.......List of credit card numbers and 800 numbers

_____

☐.......Checking account number _____

☐.......List of travelers check numbers _____

☐.......Foreign currency _____

You can get it at a good rate from an ATM upon arrival.

☐.......Small calculator (for currency conversion) __

☐☐..His ____-___-___ and Her ____-___-___ SSN

☐.......His Driver's License state____ and #_____

☐.......Her Driver's License state____ and #_____

_____

Fun Stuff:

☐☐..Camera with new batteries, big memory card

☐ ......Underwater camera (case)_____

☐ ......Video recorder with extra tapes _____

☐☐.Extra memory cards and batteries, chargers for still and video cameras _____

☐ ......Massage oil. It's your honeymoon, and they aren't your sheets!_____

☐ ......Lingerie! _____

☐ ......Lingerie! _____

☐ ......More Lingerie!_____

_____

Medical:

☐ ......Birth control_____

☐☐.Blood type: his_____her _____

☐ ......He's allergic to_____

☐ ......She's allergic to _____

☐ ......Allergy medications _____

☐☐.Doctor's name and phone number_____

☐☐.Extra copies of prescriptions and medications

☐ ......Motion sickness medication/wrist bands____

☐ ......Advil/Tylenol_____

☐☐.Sinutab/Sudafed_____

☐☐.Diarrhea/Constipation Medicine_____

Miscellaneous:

☐.......TSA approved lock and key for suitcase(s) __

☐.......Blank book for journal writing_____

☐.......Travel guides _____

☐.......Hotel phone number and address list_____

☐.......Address book _____

☐.......Postcard stamps _____

☐.......List of people to buy gifts for _____

☐.......Plastic bags for wet clothing/toiletries_____

☐☐..Swimsuits (for the beach or hotel)_____

☐☐..Travel pillows and gum _____

_____

_____

_____

Toiletries, etc.:

☐☐..Hair dryer, curling iron, rollers _____

☐☐..Shampoo, conditioner _____

☐☐..Hair gel, spray, etc. _____

☐☐..Hair brush, comb _____

☐☐..Toothbrush, toothpaste _____

☐☐ .Shaving cream _____

☐☐ .Razors _____

☐☐ .Sunscreen (SPF_____) _____

☐☐ .Sunglasses _____

☐ ......Make-up _____

☐ ......Soap pouf or loufah _____

_____

_____

_____

International travel:

☐ ......Voltage converter _____

☐☐ .Passport _____

☐☐ .Visas _____

☐☐ .International driver's license _____

☐☐ .Immunization records _____

☐ ......Foreign language dictionary _____

☐ ......Insurance information _____

_____

_____

_____

Paperwork

☐☐..Plane tickets _____

☐☐..Passports _____

☐☐..Copy 1st page of each passport (it makes replacing a lost passport much faster).

    ☐.......One copy of each in luggage. _____

    ☐.......One copy of each with someone at home.._____

☐☐..Visas _____

_____

☐☐..Copies of prescriptions _____

☐☐..Doctors phone numbers:

    ☐.......His primary care physician _____

    ☐.......Her primary care physician _____

    ☐.......Gynecologist _____

☐☐..List of traveler's check numbers (take one along, leave one with _____ at home) ____

_____

    ☐.......Both names on checks? _____

    ☐.......1st pad numbers_____to _____

        ☐...Finished on_____ in _____

    ☐.......2nd pad numbers_____to ____

        ☐...Finished on_____ in _____

☐......Credit card numbers and number to call if stolen:

    ☐......Card No._____

    Expiration_____800-_____

    ☐......Card No._____

    Expiration_____800-_____

    ☐......Card No._____

    Expiration_____800-_____

    ☐......Card No._____

    Expiration_____800-_____

    ☐......Card No._____

    Expiration_____800-_____

    ☐......Card No._____

    Expiration_____800-_____

☐......Map printouts _____

_____

_____

☐......Directions / GPS_____

_____

_____

_____

_____

Phone Numbers & Addresses

☐.......Travel Agent _____

      Phone number: _____

      Address:_____

      _____

☐.......Car rental (for the ceremony) 800-_____

      _____

☐.......Car rental (for the honeymoon) 800-_____

      _____

☐.......Hotel for night before wedding _____

      Phone number: _____

      Address:_____

☐.......Honeymoon hotel #1: _____

      Phone number: _____

      Address:_____

☐.......Honeymoon hotel #2: _____

      Phone number: _____

      Address:_____

☐.......Shuttle **him** to airport _____tel. _____

☐.......Shuttle **her** to airport _____tel._____

      _____

☐☐ . Airline for wedding 800- _____

☐ ......Shuttle **both** to airport _____ tel. _____

_____

☐ ...... Airline for honeymoon 800- _____

_____

☐ ...... Baby-sitter _____

_____

☐ ...... Pet-sitter or kennel _____

_____

☐ ...... Insurance companies _____

_____

_____

☐ ...... His parents_____

_____

☐ ...... Her parents _____

_____

☐ ......Other_____

_____

_____

_____

Final Confirmations

Two weeks before the honeymoon, by _____ .

☐.......Car rental (for the ceremony) _____

Rental agency and pick-up time: _____

Confirmation number:_____

☐.......Car rental (for the honeymoon) _____

Rental agency and pick-up time: _____

Confirmation number:_____

☐.......Hotel for night before wedding _____

Confirmation number:_____

Phone number: _____

Address:_____

☐.......Honeymoon hotel #1: _____

Confirmation number:_____

Phone number: _____

Address:_____

☐.......Honeymoon hotel #2: _____

Confirmation number:_____

Phone number: _____

Address:_____

☐.......Shuttle **him** to fly to wedding picking up at (date, time & address) _____

Phone_____Confirmation # _____

☐......Shuttle **her** to fly to wedding picking up at (date, time & address) _____

Phone_____Confirmation #_____

☐☐.Airplane reservations (wedding) _____

Departure city and time: _____

Connecting city, arrival and departure time:

Destination arrival time: _____

Airline and flight number(s): _____

Confirmation number: _____

☐......Shuttle **both** to airport for honeymoon on ___

picking up at (time & address) _____

Phone_____Confirmation #_____

☐☐.Airplane reservations (honeymoon) _____

Departure airport and time: _____

Connecting airport, arrival and departure time: _____

Destination airport and arrival time:_____

Airline and flight number(s): _____

Confirmation number: _____

☐......Buy $_____ in traveler's checks at _____

☐......Closest ATMs located at _____

☐☐.Passports valid _____

☐☐.Visas valid, immunizations current_____

Wedding Night Hotel

☐.......Preferred locations _____

_____

_____

☐.......Amenities desired _____

_____

_____

☐.......Room size desired _____

_____

☐.......First option _____

    ☐.......Location _____

    ☐.......Price _____

    ☐.......Amenities _____

☐.......Second option _____

    ☐.......Location _____

    ☐.......Price _____

    ☐.......Amenities _____

☐.......Third option _____

    ☐.......Location _____

    ☐.......Price _____

    ☐.......Amenities _____

☐ ......Fourth option_____

   ☐ ......Location _____

   ☐ ......Price _____

   ☐ ...... Amenities_____

☐ ......Final choice: _____

   ☐ ......Confirmation number _____

_____

_____

_____

_____

_____

_____

_____

_____

_____

_____

_____

_____

_____

Timelines

Every bridal magazine has them. Every wedding planner has them. This Organizer is no exception. I tried to be practical with what is included and how far in advance you should do it. Most wedding planners recommend that both moms start shopping for their dresses six months in advance. It can take quite a while to find the perfect Mother of the Bride / Groom dress, so starting to shop a full year in advance may make it less stressful for them. Plus, they have a better chance of finding a great dress on sale if they start a year in advance.

There are two pages for your actual wedding day, one for each of you. There are two reasons: (1) to make sure that you have enough time to do everything and (2) to remind you to do certain things, like eat breakfast. You might want to give it to your Honor Attendants.

There is also a page of what to do *after* your wedding. It's more than sending out thank-you notes. Among other things, you need to pick up your video, order photos (set aside several hours), and preserve/sell your gown. It's much less than you will do to plan your wedding, but you need to get it all done before you forget entirely.

The first things you must do are set a budget, decide on the formality of your wedding, and set a time frame for your wedding. Once you have a one (or two) month window, start looking at ceremony and reception sites. DO NOT DELAY LOOKING AT RECEPTION AND CEREMONY SITES. Reception sites are generally booked further in advance than ceremony sites and can generally only accommodate one wedding per day.

If you are marrying in a house of worship, meet with the officiant. They will tell you requirements and restrictions, as well as what they provide (dressing rooms, unity candleholder, Huppot).

After selecting a reception site, you should know your wedding date[4]. If you're getting married in a church or synagogue, call and confirm that you can use it the day and time you want.

The bride will probably want to start shopping for her gown too. You need to order her gown and bridesmaids' dresses AT LEAST six months in advance. If you take along ONE friend while you're shopping for your wedding dress and the bridesmaids' dresses, then you won't be overwhelmed by conflicting opinions.

Also, the bride should try on potential bridesmaids' dresses so you know how comfortable (or itchy) they are. If they are uncomfortable or look bad on you, then inflicting them on your bridesmaids is just not very nice.

---

[4] It seems somehow wrong that millions of wedding dates are decided by the availability of reception sites, but that's the way it is.

Exactly 1 Year Ahead

☐.......Mothers start shopping for their dresses.____

☐.......Visit a florist to see flowers (in-season = cheaper). _____

_____

☐.......Choose bridesmaids' dresses, especially if they are from a department store. _____

6 Months to 1 Year Ahead

☐.......Buy this Wedding Organizer. _____

☐.......Announce your engagement in local papers. Many do not print them over 1 year ahead._____

_____

☐.......Start exercising . Buy bridal magazines and carry them around. _____

☐.......Have your families meet. _____

☐.......Discuss who will pay for what, and how much they can afford (see "Budget" sheets under "Basic Information") – giving you a Budget of $ ____

☐.......Determine wedding type and formality.

    ☐.......Formal, semi-formal, informal_____

    ☐.......Non-traditional types: themed (sports, western, historical), destination (guests travel to Scotland or Lake Tahoe for the wedding), ethnic, military._____

☐ ......Choose a wedding consultant. _____

☐ ......Set a one-month time frame for your wedding. The final date may depend on reception site availability. _____

☐ ......Determine the ceremony location. _____

_____

☐ ......Select a reception site. _____

_____

☐ ......Set your wedding day._____

☐ ......Select and meet with your officiants._____

   ☐ ......Reserve the ceremony site. _____

   ☐ ......Check restrictions the site has (on secular music, birdseed, where to deliver flowers, hours). _____

☐ ......Choose your attendants. _____

☐ ......Draw up invitation lists:

   ☐ ......Yours_____# of guests _____

   ☐ ......Fiance's_____# of guests _____

   ☐ ......Her parents'_____# of guests _____

   ☐ ......His parents'_____# of guests _____

☐ ......**Don't** register for gifts yet, despite what some books say. If you register too far ahead, items may be discontinued.

_____

☐.......If you register early for engagement and shower gifts, register one place and update your registry after each party. Register more places later.

☐.......Select (good vendors book far in advance):

 ☐.......Bridal Gown!!! (at least 6 mos ahead)

 _____

 ☐.......Bustier, other undergarments _____

 _____

 ☐.......Headpiece and veil _____

 _____

 ☐.......Bridal shoes_____

 _____

 ☐.......Color scheme _____

 _____

 ☐.......Bridesmaids' dresses (at least 6 months ahead) _____

 _____

 ☐.......Photographer (candid / posed shots?)

 _____

 ☐.......Videographer _____

 _____

 ☐.......Florist_____

 _____

 _____

☐ ......Baker _____

_____

☐ ......Ceremony musician(s) _____

_____

_____

☐ ......Soloist _____

_____

☐ ......Reception DJ/band_____

_____

☐ ......If you don't already, start exercising. _____

_____

☐ ......Develop a record-keeping system for invitations, gifts, thank-you notes, etc. _____

_____

☐ ......Determine what to have each mother help with, and what you don't want any "help" with. ___

_____

_____

_____

_____

_____

4 to 6 Months Ahead

☐.......Begin attending counseling sessions with your officiant, if required._____

☐.......Check date bride will get her period the month of the wedding; if it's during the wedding or honeymoon, talk to ob/gyn about "rescheduling" it.

☐.......Order stationery. With mail order catalogs, you save on shipping and handling and may get other price breaks by ordering everything at once.

   ☐.......Invitations _____

      ☐…Lined inner envelopes _____

   ☐…Outer envelopes w/return address ____

      ☐…Response cards _____

      ☐…Reception cards _____

      ☐…Stickers to seal them (worth it) __

   ☐.......Personal stationery and notepaper ___

   ☐.......Thank you notes_____

   ☐.......Cocktail napkins, matchbooks _____

   ☐.......Thank you scrolls, cake boxes _____

☐.......Buy ___Forever stamps for thank you notes, responses_____

☐.......Buy _____stamps at ____ ¢ for invites_____

☐.......Check state marriage license requirements __

☐.......Plan your honeymoon_____

☐ ......Shop for going-away outfit[5]._____

☐ ......Have a complete physical, set blood test date, and immunizations for your honeymoon. _____

☐ ......Have your fiancé do the same. _____

☐☐ .Get passports, visas _____

☐ ......Check with the bridal shop to verify when bridal gown and bridesmaids' dresses will arrive. __

☐ ......Select a hotel for out-of-town guests and reserve a block of rooms at a reduced rate _____

☐ ......Buy ring bearer pillow, guest book, etc. _____

☐ ......Select wedding rings, request engraving:

☐ ......His: size_____, engraved _____

☐ ......Hers: size_____, engraved _____

☐ ......Enroll with bridal registries; update existing

registries. Include one national registry _____

☐ ......Update registr(ies) after each shower _____

☐ ......Reserve rehearsal dinner site _____

☐ ......Reserve groom's tuxedo (it's often free) _____

☐ ......Select attendants' gifts (his)_____

☐ ......Select attendants' gifts (hers) _____

---

[5] You won't ever wear your wedding gown out to a regular dinner, but you can wear your going-away outfit out and about.

2 to 4 Months Ahead

☐.......(e)Mail Wedding Party Information Packets _

☐.......Address wedding invitations. Have a party with your attendants so they can help._____

☐.......Set a date with your fiancé to get your marriage license. If you are in another state, ask the County Clerk if a waiver is available to get it closer to the wedding._____

☐.......Confirm you meet all religious requirements.

☐.......Alter / dry clean bridal gown. _____

☐.......Decide if you or your guests need baby-sitting services and arrange for them._____

☐.......Arrange for wedding day limousine. _____

☐.......Decide on favors. _____

☐.......Buy a wedding gift for your fiancé._____

☐.......Send GPS-able addresses for:

    ☐.......Hotel for out of town guests_____

    ☐.......Rehearsal location _____

    ☐.......Rehearsal dinner location _____

    ☐.......Ceremony location_____

    ☐.......Reception location _____

☐.......Mail international invitations_____

☐.......Decide when/if to have a bridesmaids' party, then plan it _____

☐ ......Shop for trousseau _____

☐ ......Ask more friends to assist in your wedding:

    ☐ ......Guest book attendant_____

    ☐ ......Acolyte(s) _____

    ☐ ......Reader(s) _____

    ☐ ......Bulletin/birdseed distributors _____

    ☐ ......Huppot pole holders _____

    ☐ ......Set up/check the reception site _____

☐ ......Select ceremony music (see page under Ceremony / Reception tab for all music) _____

☐ ......Select reception music _____

☐ ......Hairstylist appointments:

    ☐ ......Pre-wedding _____

    ☐ ......Wedding Day _____

☐ ......Make-up appointments, stylist and colors you like. Use the same ones your wedding day.

    ☐ ......Pre-wedding appointment _____

    ☐ ......Wedding day appointment_____

    ☐ ......Stylist _____

    ☐ ......Foundation, blush_____

    ☐ ......Eyeshadow(s) _____

    ☐ ......Lipstick/gloss/liner_____

    ☐ ......Mascara/eyeliner _____

1 to 2 Months Ahead

☐.......GET PASSPORTS AND VISAS _____

☐.......Get your marriage license_____

☐.......Final dress fitting on _____

☐.......Plan how to handle traffic, parking_____

☐.......Mail invitations_____

☐.......Make sure attendants ordered their clothing or reserved rental clothing _____

☐.......Have a formal wedding portrait done _____

☐.......Pick up wedding rings _____

☐.......Shop for your trousseau _____

☐.......Write your wedding program/bulletin _____

☐.......Write your vows, if you are doing so _____

☐.......Select readings for the ceremony:

_____

_____

☐.......Take dance classes _____

☐.......Make a list of must-have and would-like photos _____

_____

☐.......Make a list of must-have and would-like video moments_____

☐ ......Finish assembling favors. (Do you really want to do this the night before your wedding?) Ask attendants to help. _____

☐ ......Get the necessary name-change documents, if needed. _____

☐ ......Finish assembling/decorating birdseed or bubbles, or empty a bag of birdseed into a pretty basket and have guests take a handful to throw.____

☐ ......Reserve wedding night hotel room for **late**

arrival (after 6 pm). _____

☐ ......Make honeymoon reservations for:

    ☐ ......Airline_____

    ☐ ......Airport shuttle from reception _____

    ☐ ......Airport shuttle to/from hotel/resort__

    ☐ ......Hotel/resort_____

    ☐ ......Special events (shows, tours, etc.) _____

    ☐ ......Rental car _____

☐ ......Wedding gift purchased for your fiancé_____

☐ ......Attendants' gifts are purchased - his_____

☐ ......Attendants' gifts are purchased - hers_____

☐ ......Have a pre-nuptial agreement written _____

☐ ......Look at the ceremony site dressing room – does it have an iron/ironing board, mirrors? _____

_____

143

2 Weeks Ahead

☐.......GET YOUR MARRIAGE LICENSE_____

☐.......Pay all your regular bills_____

☐.......Send wedding announcements to the local papers_____

☐.......Finalize seating arrangements, write placecards _____

☐.......Final bridal gown fitting_____

☐.......Proofread your bulletins/programs _____

_____

☐.......Copy your bulletins/programs _____

_____

☐.......Gather together anything you'll need for your honeymoon that's packed away -- voltage converter, swimsuits/coats and other off-season clothing -- and put it in your suitcase(s). _____

_____

☐.......Wrap your attendants' thank you gifts_____

☐.......Keep writing thank you notes _____

☐.......Have mail held while you're away _____

☐.......Give copies of reception program to DJ/Master of Ceremonies and Reception Host/Hostess _____

Final Meetings - 2 Weeks Ahead

☐ ......Officiant _____

☐ ......Baker – give them the cake topper _____

☐ ......Caterer _____

☐ ......Reception site _____

_____

☐ ......Rehearsal dinner site _____

☐ ......Videographer – tell them any special requests _____

☐ ......Photographer – tell them any special requests

_____

☐ ......Hairdresser _____

☐ ......Make-up artist_____

☐ ......Your fiancé – nothing wedding related! **Especially** if you don't think you have the time.____

_____

☐ ......Florist _____

☐ ......Wedding coordinator_____

☐☐ . Attendants (his and hers) _____

☐ ......Your children - not wedding related! _____

_____

2 Weeks Ahead - Final Confirmations

☐.......Car rental (for the ceremony)＿＿＿＿＿

☐.......Car rental (for the honeymoon) ＿＿＿＿

☐.......Wedding hotel for bridal party ＿＿＿＿

     ☐.......Number of rooms reserved＿＿＿＿

☐.......Cancel extra rooms held by credit card on＿

＿＿＿＿＿＿＿＿＿＿＿＿＿＿＿＿＿＿

☐.......Wedding night hotel confirmed for **late arrival** (after 6 pm)＿＿＿＿＿＿＿＿＿＿

＿＿＿＿＿＿＿＿＿＿＿＿＿＿＿＿＿＿

☐.......Honeymoon hotel(s) ＿＿＿＿＿＿＿＿

＿＿＿＿＿＿＿＿＿＿＿＿＿＿＿＿＿＿

☐☐..Airplane reservations (wedding)＿＿＿＿

＿＿＿＿＿＿＿＿＿＿＿＿＿＿＿＿＿＿

☐☐..Airplane reservations (honeymoon) ＿＿＿

＿＿＿＿＿＿＿＿＿＿＿＿＿＿＿＿＿＿

☐.......Guest count in by ＿＿＿＿＿＿＿＿＿

☐☐..Haircut and styled ＿＿＿＿＿＿＿＿＿

☐.......Make-up appointment＿＿＿＿＿＿＿＿

☐.......Gown still fits (with shoes & undergarments)

＿＿＿＿＿＿＿＿＿＿＿＿＿＿＿＿＿＿

☐ ......Manicure appointment _____

☐ ......Pedicure appointment _____

☐ ......Ceremony site reserved for rehearsal _____

_____

☐ ......Rehearsal dinner site reserved _____

_____

☐ ......Baker has cake topper and is delivering cake

at____:_____to _____

☐☐ .Ring sizes: his_____hers_____

☐☐ .Rings fit and engraving is correct _____

☐☐ .Have mail held _____

☐☐ .House watched _____

☐☐ .Pets watched _____

☐☐ .Children baby-sat _____

☐☐ .Timers set on your home(s)_____

_____

☐ ......Pre-nuptial agreement finished _____

_____

☐ ......Confirm parking arrangements with the
ceremony and reception sites._____

_____

1 Week Ahead

☐.......**GET YOUR MARRIAGE LICENSE.** _____

☐.......Prepare announcements for mailing, then give them to someone to mail the day after the wedding. _____

☐.......IF YOU'RE GETTING A COLD, take Echinacea, Zinc Lozenges, Airborne™ – whatever helps you. _____

☐.......Finalize seating plan. _____

☐.......Have final consultations (via phone?) with:

    ☐.......Caterer _____

    ☐.......Florist _____

    ☐☐..Photographer, videographer _____

    ☐.......Officiant _____

☐.......Start packing for your honeymoon _____

☐.......Give a bridesmaids' party _____

☐.......Confirm rental tux style and arrival date and time. _____

☐.......Confirm rehearsal plans with:

    ☐.......Officiant _____

    ☐.......Attendants _____

    ☐.......Family members _____

☐.......Confirm hairdresser appointment(s) _____

☐.......Confirm make-up artist appointment(s) ____

☐ ......Give caterer final guest count on _____

☐ ......Confirm travel arrangements:

   ☐ ......To the wedding_____

   ☐ ......Your honeymoon _____

☐ ......**Stop** writing thank you notes until after your wedding; use any free time to relax_____

☐ ......Get a last-minute hair trim _____

☐ ......Assemble everything to:

   ☐ ......Take to the rehearsal _____

   ☐ ......Take to the ceremony site _____

   ☐ ......Take to the reception site (favors, etc.)

   ☐ ......Give attendants_____

   ☐ ......Keep in bridal emergency bag _____

☐ ......Gather your wedding clothing:

   ☐ ......Bustier/bra, underwear_____

   ☐ ......Garters, stockings/nylons_____

   ☐ ......Shoes_____

   ☐ ......Make-up_____

   ☐ ......Necklace, bracelet, earrings_____

   ☐ ......Headpiece, veil _____

☐ ......Buy a good, easy-to-read book or non-bridal magazine to read when you can't sleep (or wake up at dawn) the night before your wedding. _____

1 Day Ahead

☐.......CONFIRM THAT YOU HAVE YOUR MARRIAGE LICENSE _____

_____

☐.......Get a manicure _____

_____

☐.......Get a pedicure_____

_____

☐.......Gather non-bridal wedding day clothing:

    ☐.......Button-down shirt to wear to hair and make-up appointments so your hair and make-up don't get mussed. _____

    ☐.......Headpiece/veil to take to hairdresser appointment._____

    ☐.......Going away outfit – including shoes, socks, undergarments and jewelry._____

_____

_____

_____

_____

_____

_____

☐ ......Finish packing for your honeymoon. _____

_____

_____

_____

_____

_____

☐ ......Attend rehearsal dinner. _____

_____

☐ ......Draft anyone who comes near you to help with whatever you need._____

_____

☐ ......Socialize._____

_____

☐ ......Take a good, easy-to-read book or non-bridal magazine to bed for when you're wide awake at 3 am, 4 am,.... (It's better than counting sheep -- and you can re-read it when you're less distracted.) ____

_____

_____

_____

_____

Your Wedding Day!!! (Bride)

(Fill in approximate times in advance.)

\: .....Get up _____

\: .....Eat breakfast _____

\: .....Finish last-minute honeymoon packing _____

\: .....Shower, shave, etc._____

\: .....Have your hair done _____

\: .....Have your make-up done_____

\: .....Eat_____

\: .....Honor attendant arrives _____

\: .....Bridesmaids arrive_____

\: .....Go to the bathroom while it's still easy _____

(Put on your bustier 15-20 minutes before your gown so you can "settle" into it a bit before dressing.)

\: .....Dress_____

\: .....Limo takes you to ceremony site _____

\: .....Photos start _____

\: .....Ceremony starts _____

\: .....Photos resume _____

\: .....Reception starts _____

\: .....Reception ends _____

: ....Depart for your honeymoon _____

: ....Post-reception party with out of town guests

: ...Flight departs _____

_____

_____

_____

_____

_____

_____

_____

_____

_____

_____

_____

_____

_____

_____

Your Wedding Day!!! (Groom)

(Fill in the approximate times in advance.)

: ....Get up _____

: ....Eat breakfast _____

: ....Finish last-minute honeymoon packing_____

: ....Shower, shave, etc._____

: ....Pack toiletries _____

: ....Get dressed _____

: ....Best Man arrives_____

: ....Pick up rental car (if necessary) _____

: ....Eat_____

: ....Put on tux _____

: ....Groomsmen arrive_____

: ....Go to ceremony site _____

: .....Go to the bathroom while you have time_____

: ....Photos start _____

: ....Ceremony starts _____

: ....Photos resume _____

: ....Reception starts _____

: ....Reception ends _____

: ....Depart for your honeymoon _____

:   ...Post-reception party with out of town guests

:   ....Flight departs _____

_____

_____

_____

_____

_____

_____

_____

_____

_____

_____

_____

_____

_____

_____

_____

_____

Within 1-2 Months AFTER

☐.......Photographer: see page under "Vendors". ___

☐.......Select newspaper announcement photos. ___

_____

☐.......Submit newspaper announcements. _____

☐.......Order ____copies of your certified marriage certificate from the County Clerk (for banks, social security, etc. to change your name). _____

☐.......Open your gifts!!! We invited friends who lived nearby for a mini-party. It was a nice chance to socialize, and they recorded who gave us what so we could focus on opening. We also ate the top layer of our cake. _____

☐.......Update registries to reflect gifts you've received. You'll get a few more wedding gifts and family can buy holiday/birthday gifts from your registry. _____

☐.......Wedding gown:

    ☐.......Pick up from cleaners _____

    ☐.......Have it preserved_____

    ☐.......Take to consignment store _____

    ☐.......Hang in parents' closet for 20 years __

☐.......Buy extra photo albums._____

☐.......Wedding and honeymoon photos put in albums._____

☐ ...... **Thank you notes** sent within <u>three months</u> of return from honeymoon. For gifts of money, describing what you're buying makes writing notes easier.

    ☐ ...... Attendants (for being in the wedding, gifts, and anything specific they helped with)

    ☐☐ . Immediate family _____

    ☐☐ . Extended family _____

    ☐☐ . Bride and groom's friends_____

    ☐☐ . Parents' friends _____

    ☐☐ . Coworkers, neighbors of bride and groom

    ☐☐ . Coworkers, neighbors of parents_____

☐ ...... Videographer:

    ☐ ...... Pick up final copy of video on _____

    ☐ ...... Master tape kept until _____

    ☐ ...... Cost to buy master tape_____

☐ ...... Wedding announcement in newspapers:

    ☐☐ . His/her hometown_____

    ☐☐ . Current local paper_____

_____

_____

_____

Name Change

☐.......Social Security_____

☐ ......Car registration_____

☐.......Driver's license _____

☐.......Car title(s) _____

☐.......Passport_____

☐.......Voter registration_____

☐.......Bank(s) - checking, savings, loans - add spouse?:

      ☐☐_____

      ☐☐_____

      ☐☐_____

☐.......Student, other loans_____

☐.......Credit cards:

      ☐ _____

      ☐ _____

      ☐ _____

☐☐..IRA, 401K, other investments_____

☐.......Update lease or mortgage_____

☐.......Will_____

☐☐..College/university(s) alumni association ___

☐.......Employer_____

☐ ...... Employee records _____

☐ ...... Letterhead paper_____

☐ ...... Business cards _____

☐ ...... Email address _____

☐ ...... Phone directory listing_____

☐ ...... Insurance company(s):

    ☐ _____

    ☐ _____

☐ ...... Beneficiaries_____

_____

_____

☐ ...... Safety deposit box_____

☐ ...... Post office_____

☐ ...... Primary care physician _____

☐ ...... OB/Gyn _____

☐ ...... Eye doctor _____

☐ ...... Dentist _____

☐ ...... Other doctor _____

☐☐ . Magazines, newspaper _____

☐ ...... Club(s): _____

_____

Vendors

For your wedding, you will need to select quite a few vendors. These include the photographer, florist, videographer, reception site (see "Ceremony & Reception" section), musicians, baker, and more.

Make certain you tell vendors what matters most to you (preferably in writing) before the wedding and reiterate it on your wedding day, if necessary. In all the rushing around, sometimes even professionals forget. I absolutely insisted that photos and video be taken of our flower girls in my parent's yard. They were beautiful and meant a lot more to the family than a picture anywhere else could have.

You may choose to preserve the bridal bouquet from your wedding. Do-it-yourself methods include pressing, hanging/drying, and making potpourri. It is also possible to send your bouquet to a professional preservationist. They advertise in major bridal magazines. If you are interested in this, get brochures from each company. They have different methods for drying your flowers and then putting them in wall hangings, shadow boxes or acrylic boxes to set on a table. It's not cheap, but it's for the rest of your life and you probably spent a lot of time and money on your bridal bouquet for one day. Of course, if you don't think you'll want to display it, save your money.

If you have a Sunday wedding, verify that each vendor will work and deliver on Sunday.

Hints and Tips

- You will probably have more of your family gathered together than you have had in a long time. Don't be afraid to ask the photographer to take a few family portraits. We had pictures of each of our parents with their parents and siblings, and a second one with the siblings spouses. My cousins want copies. Just remember, unless you really stress that they are important and tell family members to seek out the photographer, they may be forgotten in the rush of events. The photographer knows who you are, but she doesn't know Aunt Gertrude.

- Remember, **these people work for you**; they are here for your convenience, not the other way around. Don't let a photographer drag you outside during dinner because "the lighting is perfect" if dinner is important to you. But don't let the caterer guilt you into finishing dinner and missing the "perfect lighting" if photos are critical to you.

- Have someone bring drinks to the bridal party during any photo shoots and make sure the caterer sends waiters out with drinks and appetizers. You probably won't even have time to stop at a water fountain. Seriously.

- When you order your wedding album, remember that all of your professional photos don't have to go in an album from the photographer. Archival quality albums cost and weigh less than professional albums and still preserve your photos. You can put some in a professional album and order more loose to put in a less expensive album.

- Professional photos are usually copyright protected, so it is illegal to make extra copies of them yourself. You will need to pay the photographer unless you have their express permission to make copies or you have bought the original files.

- Check the vendors your parents used if you're getting married in the same area. If a photography studio is still in business after 30 or 40 years, they're probably good. You'll still need to ask lots of questions, and you may not like the studio, but it's pretty cool if you do!

<u>Notes</u>

Invitations and Other Stationery

☐ ....Store or catalog_____

    ☐ ....Address _____

    ☐ ....Website _____

    ☐ ....Phone number _____

    ☐ ....Order confirmation number_____

    ☐ ....Delivery date_____

_____

_____

☐ ....Invitations and enclosures:

    ☐ ....Style ordered_____

    ☐ ....Inner envelopes _____

    ☐ ....Lining color_____

    ☐ ....Outer envelopes _____

    ☐ ....Printed flaps (worth it) _____

    ☐ ....Invitation_____

    ☐ ....RSVP with envelope _____

    ☐ ....Send RSVP to _____

    ☐ ....Envelope seals (also worth it)_____

    ☐ ....Directions to wedding_____

_____

_____

☐ ...... Directions to reception _____

_____

_____

☐ ...... Hotel information _____

_____

☐ ...... Informal notes _____

☐ ...... Announcements _____

☐ ...... Thank you notes (shower) _____

_____

☐ ...... Thank you notes (wedding) _____

_____

☐ ...... Personal stationery _____

☐ ...... Placecards _____

☐ ...... Thank you scrolls _____

☐ ...... Bookmarks _____

☐ ...... Napkins _____

☐ ...... Matchbooks _____

☐ ...... Other _____

_____

_____

Florist

☐.......Colors (to avoid clashing): attendants _____

ceremony_____and reception sites _____

☐.......Florist name _____

☐.......Address _____

☐.......Phone number _____

☐.......Time and location of delivery _____

☐☐..Bridal and toss bouquets_____

☐.......Preservation of bridal bouquet _____

☐.......Maid of Honor _____

☐.......Bridesmaids _____

☐.......Jr. Bridesmaids _____

☐.......Flower girls _____

☐.......Wreaths, sprays, etc. for hair _____

☐.......Groom _____

☐.......Best Man _____

☐.......Groomsmen_____

☐.......Jr. Groomsmen _____

☐.......Ushers _____

☐.......Ring bearer _____

☐.......Guest book attendant _____

☐☐ .Mothers (gown colors_____) _____

☐☐ .Fathers _____

☐☐☐☐ ..Grandmothers _____

☐☐☐☐ ..Grandfathers _____

☐☐ .Godparents _____

☐☐ .Special family members_____

☐ ......Organist/musician _____

☐ ......Other (officiant doesn't get one)_____

☐ ......Reception decorations _____

☐ ......Altar (take them to the reception or leave them at the church?) or Huppot flowers_____

☐☐ .Pew markers _____

☐ ......Candelabras_____

☐ ......Aisle runner (florists often provide them) ___

☐ ......Kneeler _____

☐ ......Potted flowers _____

☐ ......Table centerpieces and garlands:

    ☐ ......Bridal table_____

    ☐ ......Parent's table _____

    ☐ ......Guest tables _____

☐ ......Cake top (baker gets these) _____

☐☐ .Guest book stand, cake table_____

Florist Estimates

Estimate #1

☐.......Company name _____

☐.......Address _____

☐.......Phone number (_____)_____

☐.......Website _____

☐.......Bridal bouquet / toss bouquet_____

☐.......Bridesmaids' flowers_____

☐.......Boutonnieres_____

☐.......Altar flowers_____

☐.......Table centerpieces _____

☐.......Misc. flower_____

☐.......Delivery and set-up _____

Estimate #2

☐.......Company name _____

☐.......Address _____

☐.......Phone number (_____)_____

☐.......Website _____

☐.......Bridal bouquet / toss bouquet_____

☐.......Bridesmaids' flowers_____

☐.......Boutonnieres_____

☐ ......Altar flowers _____

☐ ......Table centerpieces_____

☐ ......Misc. flower _____

☐ ......Delivery and set-up _____

Estimate #3

☐ ......Company name_____

☐ ......Address _____

☐ ......Phone number (_____) _____

☐ ......Website_____

☐ ......Bridal bouquet / toss bouquet _____

☐ ......Bridesmaids' flowers _____

☐ ......Boutonnieres _____

☐ ......Altar flowers _____

☐ ......Table centerpieces_____

☐ ......Misc. flower _____

☐ ......Delivery and set-up _____

_____

_____

_____

_____

_____

Photographer

☐.......Photographer's name on contract _____

☐.......Studio name _____

☐.......Phone number _____

☐.......Engagement/announcement photo on_____

☐.......Wedding day arrival/departure time_____

☐.......Where will they arrive_____

☐.......Proofs ready on _____

☐.......Original files kept until _____

☐.......Can you buy original files later? _____

☐.......Can you get black and white photos too? ___

☐.......Order deadline_____for delivery on _____

☐.......Select photos for:

       ☐☐..Newspaper announcements_____

          ☐..Color _____

          ☐..Black and white _____

       ☐☐☐☐..Parents _____

       ☐☐☐☐..Grandparents _____

       ☐☐..Other gifts _____

       ☐.......Your photo album _____

       ☐☐..5x7 and 8x10 photos for home and office. _____

☐ ......Select photo album and mats _____

☐ ......Personalization for album cover_____

☐ ......Prices:

    ☐ ......Proofs (can you buy print proofs if they don't use them?)_____$

    ☐ ......4 x 5 _____$

    ☐ ......5 x 7 _____$

    ☐ ......8 x 10 _____$

    ☐ ......11 x 14 _____$

    ☐ ......16 x 20 _____$

    ☐ ......Wallets _____$

    ☐ ......Price breaks for large purchases_____

_____

☐ ......Total amount for package _____

☐ ......Amount of package cost applied toward album . _____

☐ ......Delivery date_____

Archival quality albums do not damage photos, even after many years. Albums with plastic sleeves (like archival albums) also use less space. We needed albums for table camera pictures, honeymoon photos, and professional photos we ordered loose. All the professional photos do not have to be in one album.

Photographer Estimates

Estimate #1

☐........Company name _____

☐........Photographer's name _____

The person who will photograph <u>your wedding</u>. Look at samples of <u>their work</u> and put <u>their name</u> in the contract.

☐........Address _____

☐........Phone number (_____)_____

☐........Website _____

☐........Basic cost is $_____ for ____(#) cameras and a photographer with/without an assistant. ____

for _____hours,_____photos; extra hours cost $ ____

☐........Basic package includes _____(#) photos_____

☐........Proofs available ____weeks after wedding __

_____

Estimate #2

☐........Company name _____

☐........Photographer's name _____

The person who will photograph <u>your wedding</u>. Look at samples of <u>their work</u> and put <u>their name</u> in the contract.

☐........Address _____

☐ ......Phone number (_____) _____

☐ ......Website_____

☐ ......Basic cost is $_____ for ____(#) cameras and a photographer with/without an assistant. ____

for _____hours,_____photos; extra hours cost $_____

☐ ......Basic package includes _____(#) photos _____

☐ ......Proofs available ____weeks after wedding____

_____

Estimate #3

☐ ......Company name_____

☐ ......Photographer's name _____

The person who will photograph <u>your wedding</u>. Look at samples of <u>their work</u> and put <u>their name</u> in the contract.

☐ ......Address _____

☐ ......Phone number (_____) _____

☐ ......Website_____

☐ ......Basic cost is $_____ for ____(#) cameras and a photographer with/without an assistant. ____

for _____hours,_____photos; extra hours cost $_____

☐ ......Basic package includes _____(#) photos _____

☐ ......Proofs available ____weeks after wedding____

Special Photo Requests

Ours included: my nieces in "their" flower gardens at my parents' house, a "trick" shot of Mom and me in her wedding gown (which I wore), and the cake baker and Mom (childhood friends) with the cake.

Photographers have a standard list of shots they take, but you should give them a list of anything special. Make sure they know if there are any you ABSOLUTELY WANT taken. They work for you.

☐.......First dance – if you take lessons, tell them. Also tell them if it's choreographed so they know when fancy moves like dips occur in the song. _____

_____

☐☐..Father with his parents, siblings _____

_____

☐☐..Mother with her parents, siblings _____

_____

☐☐..Multi-generational shots (great-grandma, grandmother, mother, you, sister-in-law, nieces) ___

_____

_____

☐.......Outdoor location(s) _____

_____

☐ ...... Group shots of kids _____

_____

☐ ...... Special ceremony participants _____

_____

☐ ...... Special moments (reading by a family member, song by a friend, other personalized moments) _____

_____

_____

_____

_____

_____

_____

_____

_____

_____

_____

_____

Videographer

Estimate #1

☐.......Company Name _____

☐.......Videographer's name _____

The person who would actually tape <u>your wedding</u>. You should see samples of <u>their work</u> and include <u>their name</u> in your contract.

☐.......Address _____

☐.......Phone number (_____)_____

☐.......Website _____

☐.......Basic cost is $_____ for _____(#) cameras and a videographer with/without an assistant for _____hours, extra hours cost $_____

☐.......Basic package includes ___(#) copies of video

☐.......Cost for additional copies _____

☐.......Master tape is/is not included _____

☐.......Finished video available _____weeks after wedding_____

☐.......Types of videos available _____

☐.......Special effects available_____

_____

☐.......Standard shots included _____

_____

Estimate #2

☐ ......Company Name _____

☐ ......Videographer name _____

The person who would actually tape <u>your wedding</u>. You should see samples of <u>their work</u> and include <u>their name</u> in your contract.

☐ ......Address _____

☐ ......Phone number (_____) _____

☐ ......Website_____

☐ ......Basic cost is $_____ for ____(#) cameras and a videographer with/without an assistant for _____hours, extra hours cost $ _____

☐ ......Basic package includes ___(#) copies of video

☐ ......Cost for additional copies _____

☐ ......Master tape is/is not included _____

☐ ......Finished video available ____weeks after wedding _____

☐ ......Types of videos available _____

☐ ......Special effects available _____

_____

☐ ......Standard shots included _____

_____

_____

Special Video Requests

☐.......Special moments (reading by a family member, song by a friend, other personalized moments)_____

_____

_____

_____

☐.......First dance – if you take lessons, tell them. Also tell them if it's choreographed; they should know when fancy moves like dips occur in the song.

_____

☐.......Video messages. The more you request, the greater the likelihood they won't get them all, and the less footage you'll get of other moments.

☐☐..Parents _____

☐☐☐☐..Grandparents _____

☐☐☐☐..Siblings_____

☐☐..Your children _____

☐☐..His aunts and uncles _____

☐☐..Her aunts and uncles_____

☐☐..Favorite cousins _____

☐.......Bridal party _____

☐☐..College friends _____

☐☐ . Other friends _____

_____

☐ ...... "Pan" guests during pre-ceremony music ___

_____

☐ ...... Footage of musicians performing_____

_____

_____

_____

_____

_____

_____

_____

_____

_____

_____

_____

_____

Your Marriage

Your wedding day is the first day of your married life. It's your first day as a wife or a husband. It's the biggest party in your honor that you will probably ever have.

Your wedding is not like of the rest of your life.

From the moment you say "yes" through your wedding day, everyone will focus on you. If you're the bride, they will ask about your dress and all the arrangements and admire your engagement ring. If you're the groom, they will be amazed that you're really involved in planning your wedding and will ask about her engagement ring. People will listen to you obsess over every detail down to napkin rings and the virtues of engraved versus unengraved cake knives.

This will not continue past the wedding. It can be quite a shock to go from having everyone ask you about all your plans and being the center of attention to being just another married person. This is when your marriage starts. This is necessarily not happy change for many people, even though they're thrilled to be married to the love of their life. It can be a huge change to go from being the center of attention and busily planning The Big Day, to being a regular person busy with normal household chores, or having an empty vacuum of time to fill.

If you (both of you) spend some time thinking about the things you want *after* the wedding and honeymoon are over even *before* the wedding, then you can start working toward those things as you finish your thank you notes, name changing, and other post-wedding obligations.

Think about what you spend your time on right now. How much of it is the wedding? What will you do with that large chunk of time after the wedding? Going to movies? Shopping? Watching TV reruns? Planning your future? Watching TV reruns *while* planning your future?

This section does not include all of the things you and your fiancé should talk about related to your future hopes and dreams. It won't help you make sure you have enough money to retire early or take great trips. It will, ideally, get you two to talk about your hopes and dreams for your new family. After this, hopefully you will both have the same expectations for how much you should be saving for retirement versus spending on great trips, among other things.

No one can wave a magic wand and cause you to get along with your new mother-in-law (or your own mother), but maybe discussing these things will ease a few of the potential problems. More importantly, they will help ensure that you and your new spouse are on the same page planning your lives together.

Medical History

☐.......Blood type: His_____ Her _____

☐.......His food allergies _____

_____

☐.......His medicine allergies _____

_____

☐.......His other allergies _____

_____

☐.......His chronic medical problems _____

_____

_____

_____

☐.......His hospitalizations / surgeries_____

_____

_____

☐.......His childhood illnesses _____

_____

_____

☐.......His family history of medical problems _____

_____

_____

_____

☐ ......Cancer_____

_____

☐ ......Heart conditions _____

_____

☐ ......Stroke _____

_____

☐ ......Mental health_____

_____

☐ ......Other_____

☐ ......His primary care physician_____

☐ ......Telephone_____

☐ ......His dentist _____

☐ ......Telephone_____

☐ ......His eye doctor _____

☐ ......Telephone_____

☐ ......His other doctor _____

☐ ......Telephone_____

_____

☐ ......Her food allergies _____

☐.......Her medicine allergies_____

☐.......Her other allergies _____

☐.......Her chronic medical problems_____

☐.......Her hospitalizations / surgeries _____

☐.......His major illnesses _____

☐.......Her major illnesses_____

☐.......Her childhood illnesses_____

☐.......Her family history of medical problems_____

   ☐.......Cancer _____

   ☐.......Heart conditions_____

☐ ......Stroke _____

☐ ......Mental health_____

☐ ......Other_____

☐ ......Her ob/gyn history _____

☐ ......Her ob/gyn _____

  ☐ ......Telephone_____

☐ ......Her primary care physician _____

  ☐ ......Telephone_____

☐ ......Her dentist_____

  ☐ ......Telephone_____

☐ ......Her eye doctor_____

  ☐ ......Telephone_____

☐ ......Her other doctor _____

  ☐ ......Telephone_____

Fitness / Diet

☐ ....Her food allergies_____

_____

☐ ....His food allergies _____

_____

☐ ....Foods she LOVES_____

_____

☐ ....Foods he LOVES_____

_____

☐ ....Foods she WILL NOT eat _____

_____

_____

☐ ....Foods he WILL NOT eat_____

_____

_____

☐ ....Her dietary goals _____

_____

☐ ....His dietary goals _____

_____

_____

☐ ......Exercise/sports she likes _____

_____

☐ ......Exercise/sports he likes_____

_____

☐ ......Time of day she prefers exercising_____

_____

☐ ......Time of day he prefers exercising _____

_____

☐ ......Her exercise goals_____

_____

☐ ......His exercise goals _____

_____

The question below isn't just which gym; it's running in a gym versus in the neighborhood vs while walking the dog. Exercise for its own sake or as part of daily life?

☐ ......Where she likes to exercise _____

_____

☐ ......Where he likes to exercise _____

_____

_____

Financial Planning

☐☐..Write wills_____

☐☐..Write Advance Health Care Directives _____

☐☐..Make copies and leave them with trusted family member _____

☐☐..Update insurance beneficiary information __

    ☐☐..Work policy_____

His Policy Number _____

Her Policy Number _____

    ☐☐..Non-work policy _____

His Policy Number _____

Her Policy Number _____

☐☐..Take out life insurance if you don't have any.

☐.......Buy a fire safe box; put critical documents in.

    ☐☐..Will_____

    ☐☐..Birth Certificate, incl. for children_____

    ☐☐..Passport, SSN card, incl. for children _

    ☐☐..Insurance policy _____

    ☐☐..Photos, etc., as proof for insurance ___

    ☐☐..Other _____

☐.......$..........His retirement income_____

☐.......$..........Her retirement income _____

☐ ......$ ....Combined retirement income _____

☐ ......$ ....Shortage from where you need/want

to be_____

☐ ......$ ....His monthly change in retirement

savings _____

_____

☐ ......$ ....Her monthly change in retirement

savings _____

_____

☐ ......Goal year for purchasing a home_____

☐ ......Steps needed to achieve this _____

_____

☐ ......$ ....Amount saved toward down-payment

☐ ......$ ....Amount now in non-retirement

investments _____

☐ ......$ ....Amount desired in non-retirement
investments (type desired?) _____

☐ ......$ ....His monthly change in non-retirement

Investments._____

☐ ......$ ....Her monthly change in non-
retirement investments _____

Existing Finances / Bills to Pay / Budget

Fill in the approximate amount of each bill, if you know, and which one of you will pay it each month.

☐.......$..........Gas Company _____

☐.......$..........Water and electric _____

☐.......$..........Septic/trash_____

☐.......$..........Security system_____

☐.......$..........Home Care Service – pool, maid, lawn

☐.......$..........Telephone (home) _____

☐☐..$..........Cell phones _____

☐.......$..........Cable TV _____

☐☐..$..........Car insurance _____

☐.......$..........Homeowners/renters insurance _____

☐.......$..........Engagement ring insurance _____

☐.......$..........Her retirement investments (401K,

IRA) _____

☐.......$..........His retirement investments (401K,

IRA) _____

☐.......$..........Her investments (non-retirement)____

☐.......$..........His investments (non-retirement) ____

☐.......$..........Her subscriptions_____

☐ ......$ ....His subscriptions _____

☐☐ .$ ....Newspapers_____

☐ ......$ ....Mortgage _____

☐ ......$ ....Her credit cards_____

☐ ......$ ....His credit cards _____

☐ ......$ ....Her student loans _____

☐ ......$ ....His student loans _____

☐ ......$ ....Her other loans/debts _____

☐ ......$ ....His other loans/debts _____

☐ ......$ ....Entertainment (movies, dvds, books) _

☐ ......$ ....Her lunch at work_____

☐ ......$ ....His lunch at work _____

☐ ......$ ....Other eating out _____

☐ ......$ ....Groceries _____

☐ ......$ ....Bottled water/other drinks_____

☐ ......$ ....Home repairs_____

☐ ......$ ....Other_____

☐ ......$ ....Her monthly income _____

☐ ......$ ....His monthly income_____

☐ ......$ ....Her money left after bill paying _____

☐ ......$ ....His money left after bill paying _____

Spending / Saving

When you think about Big Ticket Items, remember to include furniture, tools, major appliances, cars, a house.

$..........Her total existing debts (from previous pg)

$..........His total existing debts (from previous pg)

$..........Her total existing assets (from previous pg)

$..........His total existing assets (from previous pg)

$..........Combined existing debts _____

$..........Combined existing assets _____

_____

☐........Her just-for-fun spending_____

_____

☐........His just-for-fun spending _____

_____

☐........Big Ticket Items she really wants to save for _

_____

_____

☐........Big Ticket Items he really wants to save for__

_____

_____

☐ ......Things she is willing to "waste" money on (eating out)_____

_____

☐ ......Things he is willing to "waste" money on

(magazines) _____

_____

☐ ......Her "necessary indulgences" (Starbucks)____

_____

☐ ......His "necessary indulgences" (fancy barber)__

_____

☐ ......Items she collects _____

_____

☐ ......Items he collects _____

_____

☐ ......How many years she keeps cars for_____

☐ ......How many years he keeps cars for _____

☐ ......Her current car and anticipated replacement (type of car and how long from now) _____

☐ ......His current car and anticipated replacement (type of car and how long from now) _____

_____

Existing Accounts

Put the balance and limits for each account below to get an idea of your current financial situation. You must also decide if you will have individual or joint accounts.

☐.......His Checking Accounts (add spouse):

$..........☐ _____

$..........☐ _____

$..........☐ Business _____

☐.......Her Checking Accounts (add spouse):

$..........☐ _____

$..........☐ _____

$..........☐ Business _____

☐.......His Credit Cards (add spouse):

$..........☐ _____

$..........☐ _____

$..........☐ _____

$..........☐☐ Store Cards _____

$..........☐☐ Store Cards _____

_____

☐.......Her Credit Cards (add spouse):

$..........☐ _____

$ .... ☐ _____

$ .... ☐ _____

$ .... ☐☐ Store Cards _____

$ .... ☐☐ Store Cards _____

_____

☐ ...... His Investments (add spouse):

$ .... ☐ Ira _____

$ .... ☐ 401K _____

$ .... ☐ Other _____

_____

☐ ...... Her Investments (add spouse):

$ .... ☐ Ira _____

$ .... ☐ 401K _____

$ .... ☐ Other _____

_____

☐☐ . Car payments _____

$ .... ☐ His car _____

$ .... ☐ Her car _____

☐ ...... Monthly lease or mortgage (add spouse) ____

_____

_____

Where to Live / Ideal Home

If you don't know where you want to be, you can't get there.

☐.......Her family lives in _____

☐.......His family lives in _____

☐.......Her ideal distance from her family _____

_____

☐.......His ideal distance from his family _____

_____

☐.......Her minimum distance from his family _____

_____

☐.......His minimum distance from her family _____

_____

☐.......Her location preference (big city, town, state)

_____

☐.......His location preference (climate, hilly vs. flat)

_____

☐.......Her location restrictions (job in certain areas)

_____

_____

☐ ......His location restrictions (health problems)___

_____

☐ ......Her goal year for purchasing home _____

_____

☐ ......His goal year for purchasing home _____

_____

☐ ......Her goal size for first home_____

_____

☐ ......His goal size for first home _____

_____

☐ ......Her goal for type of first home (condo?)_____

_____

_____

☐ ......His goal for type of first home (townhouse?)_

_____

_____

☐ ......Her goal location for first home _____

_____

☐ ......His goal location for first home _____

_____

Moving In Together

☐.......Rent storage unit (If you can't agree on what is junk - store it. Work on reducing your collection of college lecture notes later.)

    ☐.......Facility name_____

    ☐.......Address _____

    ☐.......Phone number _____

    ☐.......Size and cost _____

☐☐..Plan for household goods to keep/toss. NO UNILATERAL DECISIONS. Maybe that wagon wheel coffee table has been in the family since they Brought The Wagon West – and can be hidden.____

_____

_____

☐☐..Send move-out notice _____

☐.......Sign new lease/update current lease _____

☐☐..Submit change of address to post office_____

☐.......Name for telephone listing/unlisted _____

☐☐..Disconnect old utilities on _____

    ☐☐..Gas _____

    ☐☐..Water and electric _____

    ☐☐..Security system_____

    ☐☐..Telephone (cell and home) _____

☐☐ . Cable _____

☐☐ . Septic/trash _____

☐ ......Personal space for each person _____

☐ ......New utilities connected in name of _____

starting on _____

     ☐ ......Gas _____

     ☐ ......Water and electric _____

     ☐ ......Security system _____

     ☐ ......Telephone (cell and home) _____

     ☐ ......Cable _____

     ☐ ......Septic/trash _____

☐ ......Reserve rental truck _____

☐ ......Moving helpers _____

☐ ......Confirm movers _____

☐☐ . Update address with:

     ☐☐ . Insurance company _____

     ☐☐ . DMV, employer _____

     ☐☐ . Investment companies (IRA, 401K) ___

     ☐☐ . Magazine, CD/book clubs _____

     ☐☐ . Newspaper subscriptions (cancel one?

New paper for a new city?) _____

     ☐☐ . Banks, credit card companies _____

     ☐☐ . Student and other loans _____

Religion / Kids / Family

☐.......Religion he was raised_____

☐.......Religion she was raised_____

☐.......Religion he is now _____

☐.......Religion she is now _____

☐.......How religious he is _____

_____

☐.......How religious she is _____

_____

☐.......Important religious holidays to him_____

_____

☐.......Important religious holidays to her_____

_____

☐.......Religion he wants to raise kids _____

☐.......Religion she wants to raise kids_____

☐.......Religious education he wants for kids _____

_____

☐.......Religious education she wants for kids _____

_____

☐.......He wants #_____ of kids in about _____years

☐ ......She wants #_____ of kids in about ____years

☐ ......How often he wants to visit his family _____

☐ ......How often she wants to visit her family _____

☐ ......How often he needs to visit his family _____

☐ ......How often she needs to visit her family _____

☐ ......How many years can his parents be expected to live alone, unassisted? Where will they live after that and who will care for them? _____

_____

☐ ......How many years can her parents be expected to live alone, unassisted? Where will they live after that and who will care for them? _____

_____

☐ ......Does he have any other relatives that could end up your joint responsibility? (Younger siblings, nephews, or nieces he becomes guardian of, if they're orphaned.) _____

_____

☐ ......Does she have any other relatives that could end up your joint responsibility? (Family that is elderly, infirm or has severe handicaps.) _____

_____

_____

Holidays / Special Days

This space is to record special holiday traditions you want to keep (or not!), how big (and expensive) you want them to be, and where you want to spend them (e.g., who will you see on Thanksgiving Day – or do you stay home?).

☐.......His birthday _____

_____

☐.......Her birthday _____

_____

☐.......Children's birthdays _____

_____

☐.......Wedding anniversary _____

☐.......Yom Kippur _____

_____

☐.......Valentine's Day _____

☐.......Passover_____

_____

☐.......Easter _____

_____

☐.......Memorial Day_____

☐.......4th of July _____

☐ ......Labor Day _____

☐ ......Halloween _____

_____

☐ ......Thanksgiving_____

_____

☐ ......Black Friday_____

☐ ......Chanukah_____

_____

☐ ......Christmas Eve _____

_____

☐ ......Christmas Day_____

_____

☐ ......Christmas Night _____

_____

☐ ......Day after Christmas _____

_____

☐ ......New Year's Eve_____

_____

☐ ......New Year's Day _____

_____

Traditions (Hers, His, Ours)

☐.......Birthdays _____

_____

_____

☐.......Anniversaries _____

_____

_____

☐.......Passover / Easter _____

_____

_____

☐.......Memorial Day / 4th of July / Labor Day ____

_____

_____

☐.......Halloween _____

_____

_____

☐.......Thanksgiving (incl. the weekend) _____

_____

☐ ......Christmas / Chanukah _____

_____

_____

☐ ......New Years _____

_____

_____

☐ ......Spring _____

_____

_____

☐ ......Summer _____

_____

_____

☐ ......Fall_____

_____

_____

☐ ......Winter_____

_____

☐ ......Other_____

_____

Table Assignments

Number of guests per table is _____.

Table #1

Guest #1_____

Guest #2_____

Guest #3_____

Guest #4_____

Guest #5_____

Guest #6_____

Guest #7_____

Guest #8_____

Guest #9_____

Guest #10_____

Table #2

Guest #1_____

Guest #2_____

Guest #3_____

Guest #4_____

Guest #5_____

Guest #6 _____

Guest #7 _____

Guest #8 _____

Guest #9 _____

Guest #10 _____

Table #3

Guest #1 _____

Guest #2 _____

Guest #3 _____

Guest #4 _____

Guest #5 _____

Guest #6 _____

Guest #7 _____

Guest #8 _____

Guest #9 _____

Guest #10 _____

Table #4

Guest #1 _____

Guest #2 _____

Guest #3_____

Guest #4_____

Guest #5_____

Guest #6_____

Guest #7_____

Guest #8_____

Guest #9_____

Guest #10_____

Table #5

Guest #1_____

Guest #2_____

Guest #3_____

Guest #4_____

Guest #5_____

Guest #6_____

Guest #7_____

Guest #8_____

Guest #9_____

Guest #10_____

Table #6

Guest #1 _____

Guest #2 _____

Guest #3 _____

Guest #4 _____

Guest #5 _____

Guest #6 _____

Guest #7 _____

Guest #8 _____

Guest #9 _____

Guest #10 _____

Table #7

Guest #1 _____

Guest #2 _____

Guest #3 _____

Guest #4 _____

Guest #5 _____

Guest #6 _____

Guest #7 _____

Guest #8_____

Guest #9_____

Guest #10_____

Table #8

Guest #1_____

Guest #2_____

Guest #3_____

Guest #4_____

Guest #5_____

Guest #6_____

Guest #7_____

Guest #8_____

Guest #9_____

Guest #10_____

Table #9

Guest #1_____

Guest #2_____

Guest #3_____

Guest #4_____

Guest #5 _____

Guest #6 _____

Guest #7 _____

Guest #8 _____

Guest #9 _____

Guest #10 _____

Table #10

Guest #1 _____

Guest #2 _____

Guest #3 _____

Guest #4 _____

Guest #5 _____

Guest #6 _____

Guest #7 _____

Guest #8 _____

Guest #9 _____

Guest #10 _____

Table #11

Guest #1 _____

Guest #2_____

Guest #3_____

Guest #4_____

Guest #5_____

Guest #6_____

Guest #7_____

Guest #8_____

Guest #9_____

Guest #10_____

Table #12

Guest #1_____

Guest #2_____

Guest #3_____

Guest #4_____

Guest #5_____

Guest #6_____

Guest #7_____

Guest #8_____

Guest #9_____

Guest #10 _____

Table #13

Guest #1 _____

Guest #2 _____

Guest #3 _____

Guest #4 _____

Guest #5 _____

Guest #6 _____

Guest #7 _____

Guest #8 _____

Guest #9 _____

Guest #10 _____

Table #14

Guest #1 _____

Guest #2 _____

Guest #3 _____

Guest #4 _____

Guest #5 _____

Guest #6 _____

Guest #7_____

Guest #8_____

Guest #9_____

Guest #10_____

Table #15

Guest #1_____

Guest #2_____

Guest #3_____

Guest #4_____

Guest #5_____

Guest #6_____

Guest #7_____

Guest #8_____

Guest #9_____

Guest #10_____

Table #16

Guest #1_____

Guest #2_____

Guest #3_____

Guest #4 _____

Guest #5 _____

Guest #6 _____

Guest #7 _____

Guest #8 _____

Guest #9 _____

Guest #10 _____

Table #17

Guest #1 _____

Guest #2 _____

Guest #3 _____

Guest #4 _____

Guest #5 _____

Guest #6 _____

Guest #7 _____

Guest #8 _____

Guest #9 _____

Guest #10 _____

Table #18

Guest #1_____

Guest #2_____

Guest #3_____

Guest #4_____

Guest #5_____

Guest #6_____

Guest #7_____

Guest #8_____

Guest #9_____

Guest #10_____

Table #19

Guest #1_____

Guest #2_____

Guest #3_____

Guest #4_____

Guest #5_____

Guest #6_____

Guest #7_____

Guest #8 _____

Guest #9 _____

Guest #10 _____

Table #20

Guest #1 _____

Guest #2 _____

Guest #3 _____

Guest #4 _____

Guest #5 _____

Guest #6 _____

Guest #7 _____

Guest #8 _____

Guest #9 _____

Guest #10 _____

Engagement and Shower Gift Recorder

When you've sent a thank-you note, check the box. For monetary gifts, write what you used the money for.

☐ _____

☐ _____

☐ _____

☐ _____

☐ _____

☐ _____

☐ _____

☐ _____

☐ _____

☐ _____

☐ _____

☐ _____

☐ _____

☐ _____

☐ _____

☐ _____

☐ _____

☐ _____

☐ _____

☐ _____

☐ _____

☐ _____

☐ _____

☐ _____

☐ _____

☐ _____

☐ _____

☐ _____

☐ _____

☐ _____

☐ _____

☐ _____

☐ _____

☐ _____

- [ ] _____
- [ ] _____
- [ ] _____
- [ ] _____
- [ ] _____
- [ ] _____
- [ ] _____
- [ ] _____
- [ ] _____
- [ ] _____
- [ ] _____
- [ ] _____
- [ ] _____
- [ ] _____
- [ ] _____
- [ ] _____
- [ ] _____
- [ ] _____
- [ ] _____

☐ _____

☐ _____

☐ _____

☐ _____

☐ _____

☐ _____

☐ _____

☐ _____

☐ _____

☐ _____

☐ _____

☐ _____

☐ _____

☐ _____

☐ _____

☐ _____

☐ _____

☐ _____

Wedding Gift Recorder

When you've sent a thank-you note, check the box.
For monetary gifts, write what you used the money
for.

☐ _____

☐ _____

☐ _____

☐ _____

☐ _____

☐ _____

☐ _____

☐ _____

☐ _____

☐ _____

☐ _____

☐ _____

☐ _____

☐ _____

☐ _____

☐ _____

☐ _____

☐ _____

☐ _____

☐ _____

☐ _____

☐ _____

☐ _____

☐ _____

☐ _____

☐ _____

☐ _____

☐ _____

☐ _____

☐ _____

☐ _____

☐ _____

☐ _____

☐ _____

- ☐ _____
- ☐ _____
- ☐ _____
- ☐ _____
- ☐ _____
- ☐ _____
- ☐ _____
- ☐ _____
- ☐ _____
- ☐ _____
- ☐ _____
- ☐ _____
- ☐ _____
- ☐ _____
- ☐ _____
- ☐ _____
- ☐ _____
- ☐ _____

☐ _____

☐ _____

☐ _____

☐ _____

☐ _____

☐ _____

☐ _____

☐ _____

☐ _____

☐ _____

☐ _____

☐ _____

☐ _____

☐ _____

☐ _____

☐ _____

☐ _____

☐ _____

☐ _____

☐ _____

☐ _____

☐ _____

☐ _____

☐ _____

☐ _____

☐ _____

☐ _____

☐ _____

☐ _____

☐ _____

☐ _____

☐ _____

☐ _____

☐ _____

☐ _____

☐ _____

☐ _____

☐ _____

☐ _____

☐ _____

☐ _____

☐ _____

☐ _____

☐ _____

☐ _____

☐ _____

☐ _____

☐ _____

☐ _____

☐ _____

☐ _____

☐ _____

☐ _____

☐ _____

<u>Notes</u>

About the Author

Bethanne Kim and her husband have been happily married for quite a while now. Their wedding was fun for everyone, but not really expensive, as these things go. The big shocker was that the bridesmaids could actually wear their dresses again – no joke.

She and her husband had a great vacation on their honeymoon. They didn't go to a single beach, but that's not their ideal vacation.

They have two sons, two cats, and no regrets. Well, not about anything important. (The pumpkin color hallway is best forgotten about.)

Other Books

The Constitution: It's the OS for the US describes how the US Constitution works in terms modern Americans can understand: computer terms, not legal ones. (An OS is a computer Operating System, like iOS for Apple devices.)

Survival Skills for All Ages Book 1: Basic Life Skills covers skills so simple most emergency preparedness books skip right over them. In true emergencies, knowing how to sharpen kitchen knives and basic sanitation can be literal life savers. Skills were chosen for their value in everyday life as well as emergencies.

Survival Skills for All Ages Book 2: 52+ Everyday Recipes for Emergencies is chock full of recipes that can be cooked either on or off-grid. That means that during a power outage, on a camping trip, or any other time you want or need to cook without power, you can continue to enjoy the same meals you normally have.

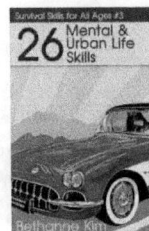

Survival Skills for All Ages Book 3: 26 Mental & Urban Life Skills covers financial skills, staying safe while traveling, self-defense, cyber security, hiding from danger, handling your emotions (including stress and anger), and more. These skills can help kids and adults throughout life, not just in school.

OMG! Not the Zombies! Book 1 A group of teens goes for a hike and accidentally starts the zombie apocalypse. Being good at being prepared, they start setting up a safe community in the old Indian cliff houses and stocking it with supplies to save themselves and their families while the adults are still pretending life is normal.

BRB! Not the Zombies! Book 2 As their group grows, they discover a new mission: Get crucial information and items to the CDC to help with efforts to create a cure for the Infection. They fight their way through zombie-infested towns and to find the "impregnable" CDC research station their hopes are pinned on.

Swept Away: Mother Nature vs. the Zombies Have you ever wondered how a hurricane might affect the zombie apocalypse? Or how the undead would fare in a sandstorm? (Hint: Hope they aren't wearing a helmet.) These and other natural disasters are explored in this series of short stories set in the same zombie apocalypse as *OMG! Not the Zombies!*

Cubmastering: Getting Started as Cubmaster is an introduction for new Cubmasters. Topics covered include organizational structure, training, recruiting, and recharter. This is about

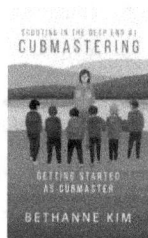

more than just the nuts and bolts of Scouting, though. It talks about dealing with difficult parents and planning special pack events.

Leader of the Pack: An Introduction to Cub Scouts focuses on the nuts and bolts of Cub Scouts. Unit organization and BSA organization are both explained, as is recharter and the various meetings (such as Roundtable) and trainings that are most common in BSA. Each chapter starts with a quote from Lord Baden Powell. Other Books

Citizenship in the World: Teaching the Merit Badge is, quite simply, a guide to assist merit badge counselors in teaching the BSA Eagle-required merit badge "Citizenship in the World." It includes the complete merit badge text and information and tips for teaching it.

Forthcoming:

Survival Skills for All Ages: 26 Outdoor Life Skills covers all kinds of camping skills such as knot tying, fire building, outdoor cooking, and choosing a tent. It also covers hunting, fishing, and foraging for food; finding your way using maps, compasses, and GPSs; and truly basic skills such as managing time and water safety (tides, currents, etc.).

Survival Skills for All Ages: Special Needs Prepping may sound like something only "other people"

need but the truth is that most families have special needs. Babies, elderly parents, diabetes, asthma, allergies – most of us have at least one of these and even if we don't, a simple sprained ankle or back injury can make us (temporarily) special needs.

Emergency preparedness can be tough, but it's even harder when someone in your family has special needs. A lot of these are surprisingly common, such as being dependent on medication ranging from an asthma inhaler or epi-pen to tightly controlled narcotics. Others, such as mobility impairment, can be long-term or short-term like a sprained ankle. Mental challenges, food allergies, diabetes, elder care, small children.... There is a lot to cover in one book

YOLO! Not the Zombies! Book 3 Follow them into the Great Plains and Texas as they continue searching not just for other survivors and their own friends and family, but for any CDC facilities that can still help fight the virus.

Contact the Author

Bethanne would love to hear from you! You can connect with her through:

Blogs–TheModerateMom.com; WiseFathers.com

Email–theWiseMom@WiseFathers.com

Facebook–The Moderate Mom

Pinterest–TheModerateMom

Twitter–@TheModerateMom

Because Amazon reviews really do matter, especially for indie authors, please take a few minutes and post a review of this book on Amazon.com.